How to Use This Book

Look for these special features in this book:

SIDEBARS, **CHARTS**, **GRAPHS**, and original **MAPS** expand your understanding of what's being discussed—and also make useful sources for classroom reports.

FAQs answer common **F**requently **A**sked **Q**uestions about people, places, and things.

WOW FACTORS offer "Who knew?" facts to keep you thinking.

TRAVEL GUIDE gives you tips on exploring the state—either in person or right from your chair!

PROJECT ROOM provides fun ideas for school assignments and incredible research projects. Plus, there's a guide to primary sources—what they are and how to cite them.

Please note: All statistics are as up-to-date as possible at the time of publication. Population
data is taken from the 2010 census.

Consultants: Callan Bentley, Assistant Professor of Geology, Northern Virginia Community
College, Annandale Campus; Sandra Jowers-Barber, Assistant Professor of History,
University of the District of Columbia; William Loren Katz

Book production by The Design Lab

Library of Congress Cataloging-in-Publication Data
Kent, Deborah.
 Washington, D.C. / by Deborah Kent. — Revised edition.
 pages cm. — (America the beautiful, third series)
 Includes bibliographical references and index.
 Audience: Ages 9–12.
 ISBN 978-0-531-28298-4 (lib. bdg.)
 1. Washington (D.C.)—Juvenile literature. I. Title.
 F194.3.K465 2014
 975.3—dc23   2013044317

CA ★ THE ★ BEAUTIFUL

Washington, D.C.

BY DEBORAH KENT

Third Series, Revised Edition

Children's Press®
An Imprint of Scholastic Inc.
New York ★ Toronto ★ London ★ Auckland ★ Sydney
Mexico City ★ New Delhi ★ Hong Kong
Danbury, Connecticut

CONTENTS

BETHESDA

SILVER SPRING

MARYLAND

Potomac

Rock Creek

Dalecarlia
Reservoir

DISTRICT OF
COLUMBIA

MARYLAND

African American
Civil War Museum

U.S. National
Arboretum

McMillan
Reservoir

Georgetown
University

International
Spy Museum

Anacostia

Lincoln Memorial

ARLINGTON

★ ◆

WASHINGTON, D.C.

The Pentagon

Frederick Douglass
National Historic Site

VIRGINIA

U.S. Capitol

ALEXANDRIA

Potomac

Oxon Run

MARYLAND

QUICK FACTS
Total area: 68 square miles (177 sq km)
Highest point: Point Reno at Fort Reno
Park, 409 feet (125 m)
Lowest point: Potomac River at sea level

0   2
Miles

Welcome to Washington, D.C.!

HOW DID WASHINGTON, D.C., GET ITS NAME?

In 1790, the United States was a brand-new nation, sparkling with promise. Its leaders planned to build a capital city on a tract of land along the Potomac River. That land was called the Federal District, or the District of Columbia, named for the explorer Christopher Columbus. And the city that would be built within the district was named for George Washington. Washington had led the 13 colonies to independence from Great Britain in the American Revolution (1775–1783). Soon he would be chosen to serve as the new nation's first president. In his honor, the nation's capital was named Washington, District of Columbia.

READ ABOUT

A view of the
Washington
Monument

LAND LAND LAND LAND LAND

CHAPTER ONE

LAND

★

MOST OF WASHINGTON, D.C., IS NESTLED ALONG THE POTOMAC RIVER BETWEEN SOUTHERN MARYLAND AND VIRGINIA. It lies on a roughly diamond-shaped snippet of land covering 68 square miles (177 square kilometers). Its highest point is 409 feet (125 meters) at Point Reno in Fort Reno Park. Its lowest point is at sea level along the Potomac. For the most part, the land in Washington, D.C., has been shaped by human hands to meet human needs and demands. In a few places, however, you can still glimpse the creeks, hills, and woodlands of the city's natural setting.

This fossil of an ancient trilobite (a crustacean-like animal that no longer exists) was found in the Washington, D.C., area.

WORDS TO KNOW

metamorphic *describing rocks that have been changed by extreme pressure, wind, and water*

magma *melted rock that has not yet erupted*

ANCIENT OCEANS AND MOUNTAINS

Hundreds of millions of years ago, an ocean covered the area that includes present-day Washington, D.C. Over time, layers of sand and mud built up on the seafloor. Later, the pieces of Earth's crust that lie beneath North America and Africa slowly smashed into each other, pushing up mountains along the east coast of North America. During the collision between the two continents, the layers of sand and mud were changed into **metamorphic** rocks. **Magma** was forced into these rocks and then cooled to form hardened rock. Over millions of years, the original mountains eroded and layers of sediment covered the coastal area.

THE LAY OF THE LAND

Most of the city of Washington is built on a flat piece of land only a little above sea level. This land belongs to

Washington, D.C., Topography

Use the color-coded elevation chart to see on the map Washington, D.C.'s high points (orange) and low points (green). Elevation is measured as the distance above or below sea level.

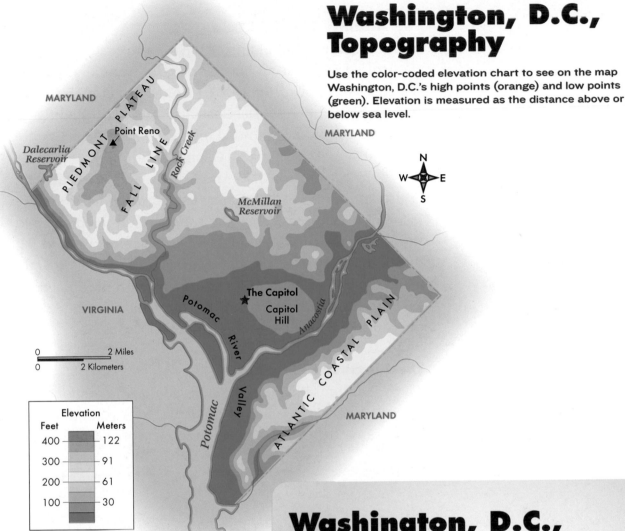

MARYLAND

MARYLAND

MARYLAND

VIRGINIA

N
W E
S

PIEDMONT PLATEAU

Point Reno

Dalecarlia Reservoir

FALL LINE

Rock Creek

McMillan Reservoir

The Capitol

Capitol Hill

Potomac River Valley

Anacostia

ATLANTIC COASTAL PLAIN

Potomac

0   2 Miles
0   2 Kilometers

Elevation	
Feet	Meters
400	122
300	91
200	61
100	30

a long, narrow region known as the Atlantic Coastal Plain. A hilly portion in the northwestern corner of the city is part of a different land region called the Piedmont Plateau. These two elements create a sense of contrast within the city limits.

Washington, D.C., Geo-Facts

Here is a list of the district's geographical highlights, including land, water, and total area.

Total area . . . . .68 square miles (177 sq km)
Land . . . . .61 square miles (158 sq km)
Water . . . . .7 square miles (18 sq km)
Inland water . . . . .7 square miles (18 sq km)
Geographic center . . . . Near 4th and L Streets NW
Latitude .38°50' to 39°00' N
Longitude . . . . .76°50' to 77°10' W
Highest point . . . . . . Point Reno at Fort Reno Park, 409 feet (125 m)
Lowest point . . . . Potomac River at sea level

Source: U.S. Census Bureau, 2010 census

The Atlantic Coastal Plain

The Atlantic Coastal Plain runs along the eastern edge of the United States from New Jersey to Florida and along the coast of the Gulf of Mexico from Florida to Texas. In Washington, the Atlantic Coastal Plain rises slightly to form a series of low, rounded hills. One of these is Capitol Hill, the site of the nation's Capitol building.

In the Washington, D.C., area, the Atlantic Coastal Plain is also known as the Tidewater. The name comes from the fact that ocean tides cause the waters of the Potomac and the Anacostia, the city's other major river, to rise and fall during the course of the day. The Potomac flows quietly along the city's western border. It joins with the Anacostia River in the southern part of the city, and it empties into Chesapeake Bay, a part of the Atlantic Ocean.

The Piedmont Plateau

The Piedmont Pleateau is a broad, fertile region that extends from New Jersey to Alabama. In Washington, it is a hilly area carved by a branching network of creeks. At

A morning fog lingers at Rock Creek Park.

one time, the Potomac River tumbled over a ledge called the Little Falls as it neared the city line. In the 1950s, a dam was built on the river, taming its flow. Below Little Falls, the Potomac makes its way between high bluffs.

Rock Creek, a **tributary** of the Potomac, flows across the city's Piedmont region. The creek and the wooded land around it are preserved as Rock Creek Park.

CLIMATE

The District of Columbia generally has a gentle climate. Winters tend to be mild, and summers are hot. But snow and sleet often snarl winter traffic, and in the days before air-conditioning, summers could be unbearably muggy and humid. Summers can also be unpleasantly wet, with one rainy day after another.

Though summer and winter have their drawbacks, few Washingtonians can find fault with spring and autumn. Warm spring days bring residents onto the sidewalks and into the parks to enjoy flowers and birdsongs. Fall days are delightful, too, with crisp breezes and colorful leaves on the trees.

WORD TO KNOW

tributary *a river that flows into a larger river*

SEE IT HERE!

ROCK CREEK PARK

Rock Creek Park is a 1,754-acre (710 hectares) slice of nature in the northwestern part of the capital. The park was created in 1890 to preserve a portion of the city's natural environment for the enjoyment of the people. The park includes a 1-mile (1.6 km) stretch of rapids along Rock Creek near the Maryland border. Farther south, the park embraces gentle hills and meadows.

Weather Report

TEMPERATURE **106°F** TEMPERATURE **-15°F**

This chart shows record temperatures (high and low) for the district, as well as average temperatures (July and January) and average annual precipitation.

Record high temperature . . . . 106°F (41°C) in 1930
Record low temperature . . . . –15°F (–26°C) in 1899
Average July temperature . . . . 80°F (27°C)
Average January temperature . . . . 36°F (2°C)
Average yearly precipitation . . . . 44 inches (112 cm)

Source: National Climatic Data Center, NESDIS, NOAA, U.S. Department of Commerce

Cherry blossoms near the
Jefferson Memorial

PLANT LIFE

In 1912, the mayor of Tokyo, Japan, gave the people of Washington a gift of friendship: Japanese cherry trees. The trees were planted in West Potomac Park, and now every spring, hundreds of thousands of people come to the park to view the lovely pink and white blossoms of the original trees and others. Another grove of Japanese cherry trees stands in East Potomac Park on an island in the Potomac River.

Many **exotic** species of trees help make the nation's capital more beautiful. Among them are ginkgos, acacias, locusts, magnolias, and ailanthuses. Many trees native to the area also grow in Washington, including pin oaks, red oaks, American lindens, and willows. Graceful American elms once adorned the parks and arched above city streets. But most fell victim to Dutch elm disease, which killed elm trees throughout the country during the 1950s and 1960s.

Washington, D.C., National Park Areas

This map shows some of Washington, D.C.'s national parks, monuments, preserves, and other areas protected by the National Park Service.

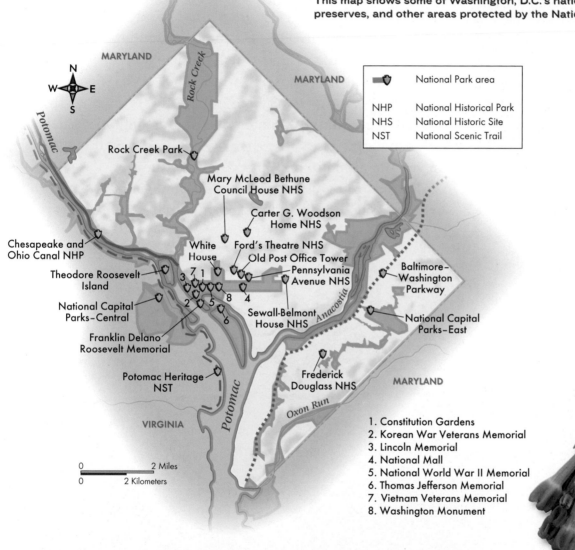

	National Park area
NHP	National Historical Park
NHS	National Historic Site
NST	National Scenic Trail

MARYLAND

MARYLAND

MARYLAND

VIRGINIA

Rock Creek

Potomac

Potomac

Anacostia

Oxon Run

Rock Creek Park

Mary McLeod Bethune Council House NHS

Carter G. Woodson Home NHS

Ford's Theatre NHS

White House

Old Post Office Tower

Pennsylvania Avenue NHS

Chesapeake and Ohio Canal NHP

Theodore Roosevelt Island

National Capital Parks–Central

Franklin Delano Roosevelt Memorial

Sewall-Belmont House NHS

Baltimore–Washington Parkway

National Capital Parks–East

Potomac Heritage NST

Frederick Douglass NHS

0   2 Miles
0   2 Kilometers

1. Constitution Gardens
2. Korean War Veterans Memorial
3. Lincoln Memorial
4. National Mall
5. National World War II Memorial
6. Thomas Jefferson Memorial
7. Vietnam Veterans Memorial
8. Washington Monument

Virginia bluebells

In spring and summer, patches of wildflowers add color to the city's parks. Jack-in-the-pulpits and pussy willows spring up in the marshes along the Anacostia. Hepaticas, bloodroots, trailing arbutuses, and many other flowers grow along the ridges in Rock Creek Park.

WHO CUT DOWN THE CHERRY TREES?

In the spring of 1999, officials began to investigate reports that vandals had cut down four cherry trees and five white cedars in West Potomac Park. The "vandals" turned out to be a small group of beavers that had found their way to Washington from marshes elsewhere along the Potomac. The National Park Service eventually trapped the beavers and moved them away from the city.

A white-tailed deer in Rock Creek Park

ANIMAL LIFE

Gray squirrels and cottontail rabbits thrive in Washington's parks. Many of the city's squirrels seem fearless and are expert at begging for peanuts and other treats. Rock Creek Park provides a habitat for white-tailed deer, opossums, raccoons, muskrats, flying squirrels, and a small number of red foxes. In the 1980s and 1990s, coyotes began adapting to city environments throughout the United States. Today, coyotes live in Washington's parks and along the city's riverbanks, but because they are active only at night, humans rarely see them.

In the spring, Washington's parks and gardens sparkle with birdsong. Cardinals, orioles, and many kinds of war-

Cardinals are among the many birds that make their homes in Washington, D.C.

blers make their home in the city. Mockingbirds are a favorite among the city's bird lovers. Hawks and bald eagles can sometimes be spotted soaring over Rock Creek Park.

Dwarf wedgemussel

CARING FOR THE LAND

Like most major cities in the United States, Washington, D.C., faces many serious environmental problems. Pollution taints its rivers and creeks, and car exhaust fumes pollute the air. To combat these problems, some 150 environmental groups formed a **coalition** called the D.C. Environmental Network. This organization increases public awareness of environmental issues and supports laws that protect the city's natural resources. It strives for a cleaner, healthier environment in the nation's capital.

WORDS TO KNOW

endangered *at risk of becoming extinct*

coalition *an organization formed by bringing together delegates from several groups*

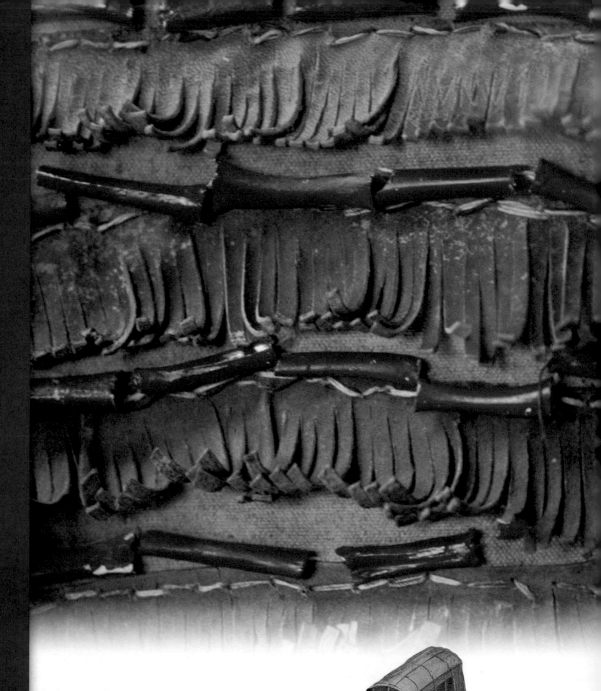

READ ABOUT

A Native American skirt made of deer skin and red painted bones

c. 10,000 BCE

The first humans reach the Potomac River

c. 8000-1200 BCE ▶

People begin living part of the year in settled villages

c. 2000 BCE

People begin carving bowls from soapstone

FIRST PEOPLE

★

IN 1996, WORK WAS SCHEDULED ON WASHINGTON'S WHITEHURST FREEWAY. Before construction got under way, archaeologists (people who study the remains of past human societies) examined the area. They investigated several sites and found jewelry made of shark's teeth, stone pendants, and a headdress of deer antlers. These items were left by some of the area's first people.

c. 1300 CE
Cooling temperatures drive northern Indians to the Potomac region, leading to warfare

c. 1500
Piscataways are ruled by a powerful chief, or tayac

1996 ▲
Archaeologists discover ancient jewelry in the Foggy Bottom neighborhood

Early peoples tend their fields, channeling water from a nearby river.

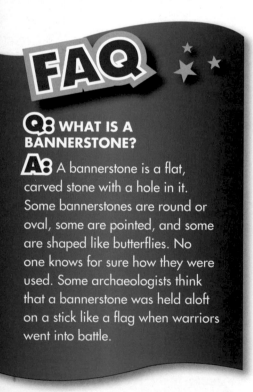

FAQ ★ ★ ★

Q8 WHAT IS A BANNERSTONE?

A8 A bannerstone is a flat, carved stone with a hole in it. Some bannerstones are round or oval, some are pointed, and some are shaped like butterflies. No one knows for sure how they were used. Some archaeologists think that a bannerstone was held aloft on a stick like a flag when warriors went into battle.

EARLIEST HUMANS

Some 20,000 years ago, a wide swath of land connected the North American and Asian continents. Nomadic hunters walked across a land bridge from what is now Siberia to Alaska in search of game. They gradually made their way across the continent, probably reaching the northern banks of the Potomac about 12,000 years ago. In the Potomac region, they hunted deer, musk ox, and other animals. They fished the rivers and streams, and gathered wild fruits, nuts, and berries.

Over time, life changed for the people along the Potomac. They eventually began raising some of their own food by planting corn, squash, and beans. They lived in settled villages during the summer months in order to tend their crops.

In about 2000 BCE, the people of the Potomac region started to carve bowls from a soft mineral called steatite, or soapstone. They also turned soapstone into beads, pipes,

Native American Peoples

(Before European Contact)

This map shows the general area of Native American peoples before European settlers arrived.

and bannerstones. Much of the stone came from a large quarry in today's Soapstone Valley east of Rock Creek.

As time passed, settlers along the Potomac learned to make pottery from clay they dug on the riverbanks. They shaped wet clay into bowls and jars, which they dried in

This Algonquian village in what is now Virginia has houses arranged in a circle.

the sun. They discovered that heating the pottery in a fire gave it added strength.

THE PISCATAWAY PEOPLE

Native Americans known as Piscataways probably descended from early hunters who lived along the Potomac. Piscataways were Algonquians, a larger group that shared similar customs and had related languages.

The Piscataway people lived in villages along rivers and creeks. The women planted and cared for the crops.

The men hunted with bows and arrows, fished, and cleared fields. Piscataways lived in houses made of bent saplings covered with woven mats. Each house was long and narrow. Sometimes several families lived in one large house.

During the 1300s, the climate of eastern North America grew colder. Other peoples from farther north moved south to Piscataway territory, where game was more plentiful. Fighting quickly flared between the newcomers and Piscataways. For the next 300 years, Piscataways were often at war with Susquehannocks and other neighboring peoples.

To resist the invaders, various Piscataway groups united under a strong chief, or *tayac*. Lesser chiefs, called *weroances*, headed villages. Each weroance collected gifts, or **tribute**, from his people. The weroance then brought tribute to the tayac. In return for these gifts, the tayac protected the many Piscataway villages.

THE WORLD OF SPIRITS

Piscataways believed that spirits dwelled within every natural object and living thing. The sun, moon, clouds, and streams all had powerful spirits. So did the trees, flowers, fish, hawks, deer, foxes, and other animals. When a Piscataway hunter killed an animal for food, he thanked its spirit for feeding the people.

The people used prayers and ceremonies to keep the spirits happy. Piscataway healers were believed to have a special ability to communicate with the spirits. They performed ceremonies to ensure good crops and to heal the sick.

These ceremonies could do nothing to stop the dramatic changes that would alter the world of the Piscataways. In the 1600s, pale-skinned strangers would arrive in Piscataway lands, changing their way of life forever.

tribute *gifts given to a leader in exchange for protection*

THE THREE SISTERS

According to an Indian legend, a band of Susquehannocks once surrounded a Piscataway village on the Potomac. Three young Piscataway men set out in a canoe to catch fish to feed the village, but Susquehannocks killed them. Their sweethearts, the daughters of a healer, set out on a raft to avenge the young men's deaths. But their raft overturned in the swift current, and the three women saw that they would not reach the Susquehannock camp. Before they drowned, they swore that no one would ever be able to cross the river at that spot. The three women were turned into rocky islands known today as the Three Sisters. All attempts to build a bridge near the Three Sisters have failed. Some say the failures are a result of the curse the young women placed on that spot long ago.

READ ABOUT

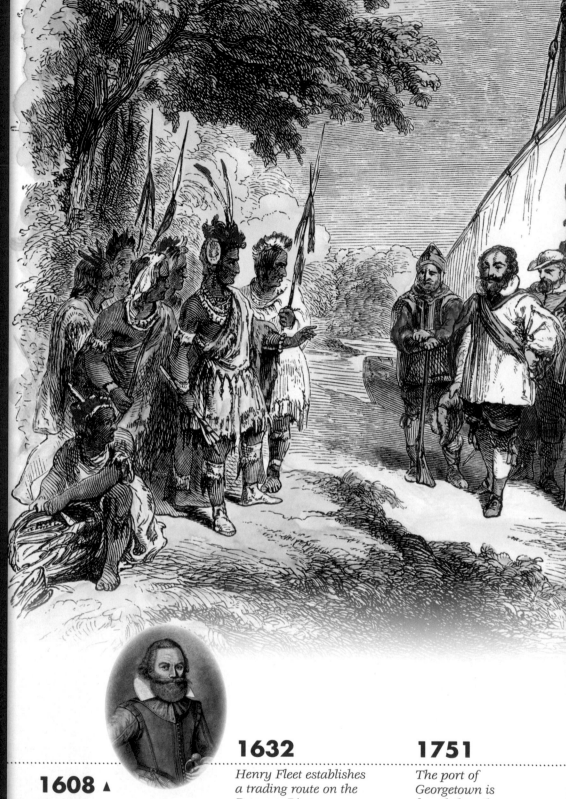

John Smith meeting with Native Americans in Virginia Colony

1608 ▲

John Smith sails up the Potomac River

1632

Henry Fleet establishes a trading route on the Potomac River

1751

The port of Georgetown is founded on the Potomac

CHAPTER THREE

EXPLORATION AND SETTLEMENT

★

IN 1608, JOHN SMITH SAILED UP THE POTOMAC RIVER WITH A SMALL EXPLORING PARTY. He was the leader of Jamestown, an English settlement in present-day Virginia, about 150 miles (241 km) to the south. Smith visited the village of Nacochtanke, where he and his men received a gracious welcome from the Piscataways. Though Smith did not stay long, his visit marked the beginning of changes for the Piscataways.

1790 ►

President George Washington selects the site for Washington, D.C.

1800

Congress and the president move into Washington, making it the official seat of government

1814

British troops burn Washington during the War of 1812

The Ark and the Dove

EDWIN TUNIS

WORDS TO KNOW

immunity *protection against disease*

indentured servants *people who work for others under contract*

THE FOUNDING OF MARYLAND

In 1632, Henry Fleet, an English fur trader from the Jamestown Colony, established a trading route on the Potomac River. He offered the Indians guns, kettles, beads, and other goods in exchange for beaver pelts. Fleet was probably the first European to live on the land that is now Washington, D.C.

The next year, two ships set sail from England. The *Ark* and the *Dove* carried a total of about 140 passengers bound for the wilderness north of the Potomac. The ships reached Chesapeake Bay in March 1634. With the help of Fleet, who spoke the Piscataway language, the newcomers bought a tract of land from the Indians. There they established St. Mary's, the first European town in present-day Maryland.

At first, the Piscataway people welcomed the newcomers. They thought the English colonists would be strong allies against their enemies, the Susquehannocks. As more and more colonists arrived, however, they drove the Piscataways off their land. The Indians also fell prey to smallpox, measles, and other European diseases. Native Americans had never been exposed to these illnesses before and had no natural **immunity** to them. The diseases wiped out entire villages. By 1700, most of the surviving Piscataways had moved north out of the area.

The English divided much of early Maryland into large estates for growing tobacco. One such estate, Duddington Manor, was located on land that is now part of the District of Columbia. The tobacco growers and their families enjoyed a comfortable lifestyle, much like that of the English upper class. They organized horse races, and lavish parties.

Indentured servants and enslaved workers did most of the work on the estates. People who became indentured

European Exploration of Washington, D.C.

The colored arrows on this map show the routes taken by explorers between 1608 and 1634.

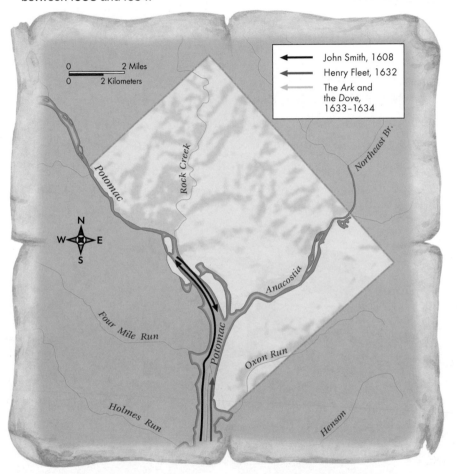

←	John Smith, 1608
←	Henry Fleet, 1632
←	The *Ark* and the *Dove*, 1633–1634

servants had wanted to move to the colony but could not afford the ship's fare. They agreed to work without wages for up to seven years for the person who paid their fare. Most of the enslaved people in Maryland were people of African descent. They had been kidnapped from Africa and shipped to the West Indies or to the British colonies in North America. Unlike indentured servants, enslaved workers were considered property. They could be bought and sold and were enslaved for life. Any children they had were also enslaved.

Maryland's tobacco growers were eager to expand their trade and believed that their colony needed its own port city. In 1751, they founded Georgetown on the Potomac River west of Rock Creek. Across the Potomac in Virginia stood another port, Alexandria.

A NATION AND A CAPITAL

In the 1760s and 1770s, Great Britain imposed a series of taxes on its colonies in North America to help pay for its army. The Americans protested these taxes, complaining that they were unfair because the colonies had no

American forces and British troops fighting in the Battle of Yorktown, 1781

Washington, D.C., and the Colonies

This map shows the original 13 colonies and the previous two capitals of the United States.

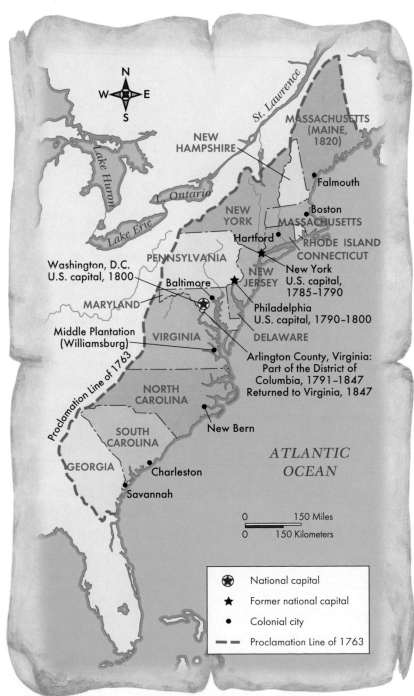

representatives in the British Parliament to speak for them. They called this taxation without representation. Tensions grew, and in 1775, the American Revolution began. When the war ended in 1783, the colonies achieved independence, a new nation had been born: the United States of America.

In the beginning, the former colonists were not sure how to govern themselves. They could not even agree on what city should serve as their capital. Soon after the Revolution, New York City served as the nation's capital. Then the capital shifted to Philadelphia, Pennsylvania. People in the South hoped for a capital in one of the southern states, while northerners argued that the capital should be in a state such as New Jersey, New York, or Pennsylvania.

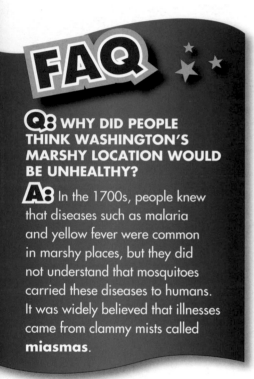

WORDS TO KNOW

miasmas *thick, clammy mists hanging over a marsh*

surveyor *someone whose job is to find the shape and position of an area of land*

George Washington, the nation's first president, imagined the capital as a grand port for trading goods. He wanted the capital city to be built somewhere along the Potomac River, which lay almost midway between the northern and southern states. Washington's plan was accepted in 1790.

For three weeks, Washington and his assistants rode up and down the Potomac, searching for the proper site. At last, Washington announced that the new capital city would be built on a diamond-shaped tract of land covering 100 square miles (259 sq km) that included the port of Georgetown. Most of the land would be purchased from the state of Maryland. A small piece, including the town of Alexandria, would be purchased from Virginia. (This section, about a third of the original area, was returned to Virginia in 1847.)

Some people protested that the site was unsuitable for a major city. Part of the land was marshy and likely to be unhealthy. Congress, however, approved the location. Plans for building the new city got under way.

To oversee construction of the new capital, Washington appointed three commissioners: Daniel Carroll, Thomas Johnson, and David Stuart. He also appointed a young French **surveyor** named Pierre-Charles L'Enfant to draw up plans for the new city. L'Enfant had designed Federal Hall in New York City, the building where Washington had been sworn in as president. Washington stated that L'Enfant was "better qualified than anyone who had come within my knowledge in this country, or indeed in any other."

L'Enfant was a man of grand ideas. As he studied the hills and fields where the new city would stand, he imagined stately buildings, dazzling monuments, sparkling fountains, and broad, sweeping boulevards. He drew

Creating Washington, D.C.

This map shows the states of Virginia and Maryland and the land they contributed to create Washington, D.C.

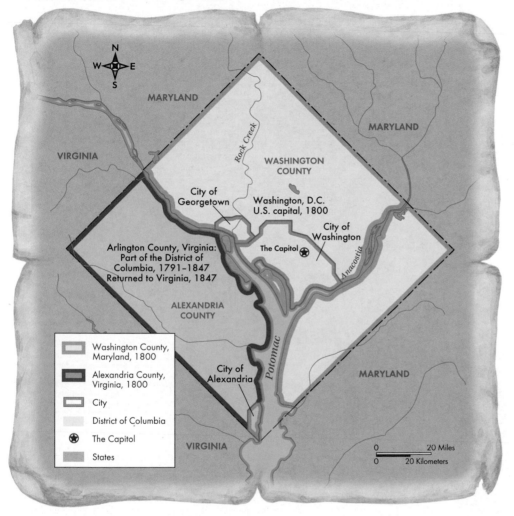

plans for a city with a grid of streets and wide, tree-lined avenues radiating from the center. Wherever the streets and avenues crossed, he planned circles or squares where monuments could be placed. A spot called Jenkins Hill, he decided, was an ideal place for the federal Capitol. L'Enfant described the hill as "a pedestal waiting for a monument." It is now known as Capitol Hill.

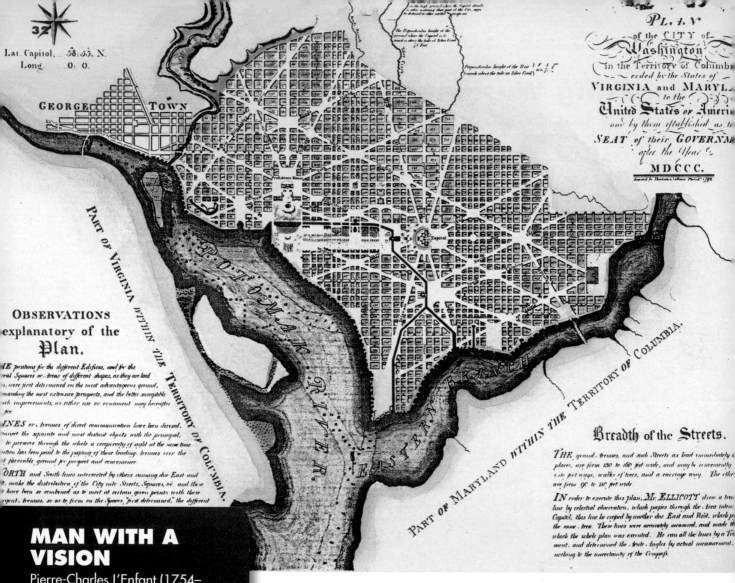

Lat. Capitol... 38.53. N.
Long. ...0: 0.

GEORGE TOWN

PART OF VIRGINIA WITHIN THE TERRITORY OF COLUMBIA.

OBSERVATIONS
explanatory of the
Plan.

POTOMAK RIVER.

EASTERN BRANCH.

PART OF MARYLAND WITHIN THE TERRITORY OF COLUMBIA.

PL. IV
of the CITY of
Washington
in the Territory of Columbia
ceded by the States of
VIRGINIA and MARYL
to the
United States of Ameri
and by them established as the
SEAT of their GOVERNM
after the Year
MDCCC.

Breadth of the Streets.

MAN WITH A VISION

Pierre-Charles L'Enfant (1754–1825) was born in France and came to North America to fight with the rebelling colonies in the American Revolution. He designed Federal Hall in New York City and was hired to lay out the U.S. capital on the Potomac. L'Enfant made plans for a magnificent city with wide boulevards, but because of a series of quarrels with local landowners, he was fired in 1791. L'Enfant died in poverty, but his grand plan for the city endured.

Andrew Ellicott's engraved map from 1792, based on the original plans created by Pierre-Charles L'Enfant

The federal government agreed to pay landowners $66 per acre (0.4 ha) for the land used in constructing the capital city. But the owners would not be paid for land that was used for streets and avenues. When they learned about L'Enfant's plans, the landowners were outraged. The grand boulevards would be 160 feet (49 m) wide! It wasn't fair, they argued, that they should give up so much of their farmland without receiving payment in return.

President Washington calmed the landowners, but within a few months more trouble flared up. Commissioner Daniel Carroll began work on a new manor house. Unfortunately, Carroll's house jutted into one of the avenues that L'Enfant was planning. L'Enfant told Carroll to move the manor house away from the avenue or tear it down.

Carroll, one of the wealthiest people in the area, was not used to taking orders from a mere surveyor, and he refused to change the location of his house. Furious, L'Enfant ordered his work crew to tear down part of the house.

Carroll complained to the president. Washington respected L'Enfant but thought he had gone too far. He fired L'Enfant and commanded him to turn over the plans he had drawn up. L'Enfant refused to hand over his work.

Washington hired a new surveyor, Andrew Ellicott, to complete the plans for the capital. Ellicott had worked with L'Enfant and had a rough idea of his design, but without L'Enfant's original plans he feared he would have to make a fresh start.

According to legend, one of L'Enfant's former assistants, Benjamin Banneker, came to the rescue. A free African American, Banneker had seen L'Enfant's plans and managed to reproduce them entirely from memory. Some historians question this story and claim that

MINI-BIO

BENJAMIN BANNEKER: MAN OF MANY GIFTS

Benjamin Banneker (1731–1806) was the son of a free African American mother and an enslaved father. His mother eventually purchased his father's freedom. Banneker showed remarkable ability in mathematics and an unending curiosity about the stars and planets. He became a noted mathematician and astronomer. From 1792 to 1797, Banneker published a yearly almanac filled with information about the weather, the stars, and farming. But he is best remembered for assisting surveyors Pierre-Charles L'Enfant and Andrew Ellicott in designing the U.S. capital.

 Want to know more? Visit www.factsfornow.scholastic.com and enter the keywords **Washington D.C.**

Ellicott's brother Benjamin had re-created L'Enfant's original design. Like Banneker, Benjamin Ellicott had worked closely with L'Enfant and had seen his drawings.

Under the direction of Andrew Ellicott and Banneker, work on the capital city moved forward. It followed much of L'Enfant's design, and the result was a city of wide avenues with plenty of space for the monuments and splendid buildings of the future.

CONSTRUCTION BEGINS

L'Enfant envisioned a splendid boulevard sweeping through the heart of the capital. At one end would stand the president's mansion. At the other end would be the Capitol, where Congress would hold its sessions. L'Enfant did not have time to design these key buildings. The commissioners were left with the task of finding architects to carry out these projects.

In 1792, the commissioners offered a $500 prize and a small piece of land in the capital city to the person who submitted the best design for the Capitol. They received several entries but did not like any of them. The contest deadline came and went, with nothing accomplished.

Several months after the contest ended, the commissioners received an entry from William Thornton, a doctor who was originally from Great Britain. He suggested a building with a domed **rotunda** flanked by north and south wings for the House of Representatives and the Senate. President Washington liked the plan immediately, praising its "grandeur, simplicity and convenience." Washington and the commissioners approved the plan. Construction of the Capitol officially began on September 18, 1793.

Construction was a daunting project. The site for the Capitol had to be cleared and smoothed. Workers cut

WORD TO KNOW

rotunda *a large, round room*

George Washington laying the cornerstone
for the Capitol in 1793

huge blocks of sandstone from a quarry in Aquia, Virginia, and hauled them to the building site by ferry and wagon. Others cut massive wooden beams and baked thousands of bricks. About 600 laborers did the actual work of building the Capitol. According to records, around 400 of these workers, many of them highly skilled, were enslaved Africans. Their owners in Maryland, Virginia, and the District of Columbia received five dollars a month for their work on the Capitol project.

Picture Yourself . . .

Building the U.S. Capitol

Your father warns you to back away as workers wrestle a huge block of stone off a wagon. Their muscles bulge as they slide the mighty stone onto the ground. Your father inspects it carefully. He walks around it to see it from every angle and studies it with his practiced hands. The stone is rough and jagged, but he will shape it with his hammer and chisel until it matches the others that lie nearby. He and the other stonemasons know how to trim these massive rocks so that they will fit together perfectly.

You hope you can master these skills yourself. Your father says it's a matter of practice. He hands you a chisel and shows you how to chip away bits of stone. Using a heavy hammer, your father breaks away great, uneven chunks. Slowly, stone by stone, the wall of the new Capitol rises before you. It will stand long after you and your father and all of these workers are gone. Maybe someday, people will gaze at it and wonder who carved the stones to build walls that would last for centuries to come.

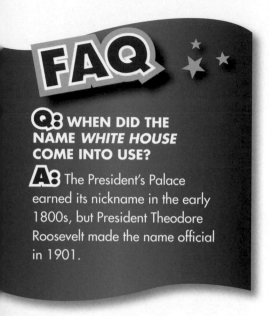

FAQ

Q: WHEN DID THE NAME *WHITE HOUSE* COME INTO USE?

A: The President's Palace earned its nickname in the early 1800s, but President Theodore Roosevelt made the name official in 1901.

The east side of the President's Palace, later known as the White House, as it appeared in 1807

At the other end of L'Enfant's grand boulevard, work on the President's Palace got under way. Like the Capitol, the President's Palace was built largely by enslaved laborers. Free African Americans also worked on both buildings.

Congress was supposed to move into the Capitol in 1800, but problems plagued the construction. Lacking sufficient money to complete the building by that year, they decided to finish the north wing and let the rest be completed later.

EARLY DAYS IN WASHINGTON

In June 1800, a procession of horse-drawn wagons clattered into the District of Columbia. The wagons carried the household goods of President John Adams and other employees of the U.S. government—more than 100 people in all. They also brought boxes packed with all the official

documents that the nation had accumulated in its brief history. The federal government was taking up residence in the brand-new capital.

On November 1, 1800, John Adams became the first president to occupy the President's Palace. The building was still under construction. It was surrounded by brick-yards and heaps of rubble. Inside, many of the rooms were bare and unfinished. When Abigail Adams arrived a few weeks later, her laundry was hung to dry in the palace's East Room. The Capitol, too, remained under construction. When Congress met in the North Wing on November 22, busy workers still sawed and hammered in other parts of the building.

The Washington of 1800 shared little of L'Enfant's grand vision. Of the 300 streets that L'Enfant had planned, only three were completed. Cows grazed along what later became broad avenues. Much of the rest of the city amounted to cornfields, pigpens, and scattered houses. Yet the newcomers managed to see beyond their rough surroundings. Entering the new capital of a new nation, they shared excitement and hope.

In 1804, the city council of the District of Columbia passed an act to establish a system of public education. Two small wooden schoolhouses opened in 1806. **Segregation** was the rule in Washington, D.C., from the start. At first, public schools in the district were only for white children. Public schools for black children finally opened in 1862.

THE CITY IN FLAMES

In 1810, the U.S. attorney general described Washington as "a meagre village, a place with a few bad houses and extensive swamps." Yet the capital city also enjoyed a taste of high society. Wealthy residents held parties and

THE PEOPLE OF THE CAPITAL

In 1800, three-quarters of all Washingtonians were white and one-quarter were African American. More than 80 percent of the African Americans were enslaved, and the rest were free.

WORD TO KNOW

segregation *separation from others, according to race, class, ethnic group, religion, or other factors*

Thomas Jefferson, the third president of the United States, was the first president of the Board of Trustees of Public Schools in Washington, D.C.

British troops burning the White House during the War of 1812

dances. Dolley Madison, the wife of the fourth president, James Madison, was a lively hostess. Foreign officials and members of America's upper classes flocked to dinners and receptions at the President's Palace.

But trouble was on the horizon. British and U.S. naval ships vied for power on the high seas. The hostilities flared into what is called the War of 1812.

On August 24, 1814, a poorly trained band of American **militia** tried to resist a British assault on the town of Bladensburg, Maryland. The British routed the Americans. With the militia in full retreat, British forces marched toward the undefended capital.

With the British heading their way, Washingtonians flew into action. Government workers moved important documents to safety. Elias Boudinot Caldwell, a clerk at the Supreme Court, managed to move the court's library of 3,000 books to his house.

President Madison had rushed away from the capital to see what was happening in Bladensburg. At the President's Palace, Dolley Madison waited anxiously for news from her husband. At last, two dust-covered messengers arrived, urging her to flee before the British stormed the city. At 3 P.M., she wrote to her sister, "Here I am still, within sound of the cannon. . . . A wagon has been procured, and I have had it filled with plate [silverware] and the most valuable portable articles belonging to the house. . . . I insist on waiting until the large picture of General Washington is secured. . . . I have ordered the frame to be broken and the canvas taken out. It is done. . . . And now, dear sister, I must leave this house."

That night, the British army marched into Washington. The

WORD TO KNOW

militia *an army made up of citizens trained to serve as soldiers in an emergency*

Dolley Madison saving a portrait of George Washington from the White House as British forces approach

soldiers found the city nearly deserted, so they got to work setting the capital's public buildings ablaze. The Capitol was first. The soldiers piled furniture in the North Wing to build a bonfire. Skylights and chandeliers melted in the intense heat, and great marble columns cracked. Then, with a terrible roar and shower of flames, the roof fell in.

From the Capitol, the army marched to the President's Palace. Mary Hunter, one of the few residents remaining in the city, wrote, "No pen can describe the appalling sound that our ears heard and the sight that our eyes saw."

At the President's Palace, the soldiers feasted on the president's food and grabbed souvenirs of their conquest. Then, using furniture for kindling, they set the mansion on fire. Soon, only the outer walls were left standing.

Throughout the night and during the following day, the British set fires and watched the city burn. After burning the city's public buildings, the British withdrew.

REBUILDING THE CITY

Over the next few months, the Americans defeated the British in a series of crushing battles, and in December the two sides signed a peace treaty.

But the capital city was in ruins. Some members of Congress wanted to abandon Washington and move the capital to another city. After much discussion, however, the majority voted to rebuild Washington on the site George Washington had chosen.

James and Dolley Madison never lived in the President's Palace again. Colonel John Tayloe, a wealthy Virginian, invited them to live in the Octagon House, a home he owned in the capital. After three years of reconstruction, the President's Palace was ready to be occupied again. It became the home of President James Monroe and his wife, Elizabeth, in 1817.

SEE IT HERE!

OCTAGON HOUSE

William Thornton, who drew the prize-winning plan for the U.S. Capitol, also designed the Octagon House. Completed in 1801, the house served as the winter home of wealthy Virginian John Tayloe III. After the War of 1812, it was home to President James Madison and his wife, Dolley. Today, the Octagon House is the site of a museum on architecture operated by the American Architectural Foundation.

A view of Washington, D.C., from the President's Palace, 1820

The Capitol was unfinished when the British attacked in 1814, and after the attack it was so badly damaged that it could not be used at all. For a few months, Congress met at Blodgett's Hotel. Between 1815 and 1819, Congress held its sessions in a three-story brick building on First Street in the city's northeast section, where the Supreme Court stands today.

With fierce determination, the people of Washington cleared away the rubble of the fires of 1814. Little by little, they rebuilt their homes and public buildings. The work was slow and costly, but the city of Washington began to rise again.

READ ABOUT

This is how the U.S. Capitol and the surrounding city appeared in the late 1800s.

1848 ▲
Work begins on the Washington Monument

1850
The Compromise of 1850 ends the sale of slaves in Washington

1855
The Smithsonian Institution Castle opens to the public

CHAPTER FOUR

GROWTH AND CHANGE

★

P RESIDENT GEORGE WASHINGTON HAD IMAGINED THE NATION'S CAPITAL AS A BOOMING CENTER OF INDUSTRY AND TRADE. Yet by the 1820s, Washington had only one major business—the federal government. As the young nation grew and prospered, its capital grew in power and importance.

1861–1865

Washington serves as a supply station for the Union army during the Civil War

1865 ►

Abraham Lincoln is assassinated at Ford's Theatre

1874

Congress ends home rule in Washington

Enslaved Africans for sale, early 1800s

LIVING IN THE CAPITAL

In 1820, Washington was rough and unfinished yet lively and sophisticated. Women and men in elegant dress attended balls, receptions, and theater parties. People flocked to the city from all over the country to meet with government officials. Diplomats spoke French, German, and Italian in the streets, bringing a European flavor to the rough capital on the Potomac.

Yet beneath the bustle and glitter lurked the stark reality of slavery. Many of the city's wealthy families owned enslaved Africans who cooked, cleaned house, washed clothes, and cared for children. Enslaved laborers drove carriages, scrubbed stables, and unloaded cargo on the docks. As a center for the domestic slave trade, Washington had several slave markets, where human beings were bought and sold. It also had many jails for slaves.

Free African Americans in Washington worked at a variety of trades. Some drove wagons, and others ran small businesses. Others were barbers, maids, carpenters, bakers, and shopkeepers. A set of strict laws called the Black Codes limited the rights and freedoms of African Americans in Washington. For example, blacks could be fined if they were out after 10 P.M. Despite these restrictions, a black middle class began to grow and prosper in the city.

WASHINGTON UNDER CONSTRUCTION

Scaffolds and builders' rubble were a way of life in Washington from the time it was founded. In the decades after the War of 1812, construction seemed endless. President Andrew Jackson ordered major work done on the White House. Under his direction, the East Room, where Abigail Adams's laundry once hung, became a magnificent ballroom.

In 1848, construction began on a monument to George Washington. The Washington Monument was part of L'Enfant's original design for the city. In 1851, workers started enlarging the Capitol to meet the needs of the ever-growing government.

Picture Yourself . . .

Moving to the Capital

You and your parents have just arrived in Washington from Philadelphia. Now you take a carriage across the city to meet your uncle, who works in the Treasury Department. You can't believe how bad the roads are in the capital city! Your carriage bounces over unpaved streets, weaving its way among stumps and boulders. The horses' hooves kick up mud that spatters your face and clothes. Then, with a sickening jolt, a wheel gets stuck in a pothole, and you are nearly tipped onto the ground. When you see your uncle, you're going to ask him why the Treasury Department can't pay to get the streets fixed!

SLAVE PENS

Enslaved people who were for sale were kept in pens or jails for inspection by prospective buyers. An enslaved man named Solomon Northup described his experience in a Washington slave pen in 1841. "Strange as it may seem," Northup wrote, "within plain sight of this same [pen], looking down from its commanding height upon it, was the Capitol. The voices of patriotic representatives boasting of freedom and equality, and the rattling of the poor slave's chains, almost commingled."

CASTING FREEDOM'S STATUE

When Thomas Crawford's plaster model of Freedom arrived in Washington, it had to be cast in bronze at a **foundry**. The government hired Clark Mills, a sculptor and foundry owner from South Carolina, to supervise the work. Mills brought along a master builder named Philip Reid. Though Reid was himself enslaved, he played a key role in casting and assembling the massive sections of the statue of Freedom.

WORDS TO KNOW

foundry *a building where metals are cast*

abolition *a legal end to slavery*

An Englishman's unexpected legacy launched another construction project in the capital. James Smithson never set foot in the United States, but he admired the young nation. He left his fortune "to the United States of America, to found at Washington . . . an establishment for the increase and diffusion of knowledge among men." The money reached the United States in 1838, more than $500,000 in 11 boxes of gold coins. In today's age of billion-dollar budgets, $500,000 may not sound remarkable, but in 1838 it was one of the largest fortunes in the world.

For years, scientists, scholars, and government officials debated how Smithson's extraordinary gift should be used. At last, it was decided that an institution should be founded that would serve as a museum and research center. Work on the Smithsonian Institution Building, known as the Castle, began in 1847. The Castle, the first building of the vast Smithsonian complex, opened its doors in 1855.

THE CALL TO FREEDOM

In 1855, work on the U.S. Capitol was nearly complete. The building needed a statue to crown its dome. Thomas Crawford, an American sculptor living in Rome, was commissioned to design a statue that would represent freedom. He designed a female figure wearing a cap.

During the 1830s and 1840s, growing numbers of people in Northern states, and some in the South as well, spoke out against slavery. Many whites and free African Americans insisted that slavery should be ended, or abolished. Most states in the North had passed laws for the gradual emancipation, or freeing, of enslaved people. But slavery was deeply embedded in the economy of the South. Cotton and tobacco planters feared they could not raise their crops without slave labor. They saw the **abolition**

An illustration of the Smithsonian Institution building, late 1800s

movement as a threat to their profits and fought to maintain the slavery system.

In 1850, Congress passed a law leaving to the individual state governments the decision of whether or not to allow slavery in new western states that joined the Union. This law was part of the Compromise of 1850, which also ended the sale of enslaved people in Washington, D.C. People in Washington could still own slaves, however, and they could buy them elsewhere and bring them into the capital. In 1860, some 3,185 enslaved men, women, and children lived in Washington.

Abraham Lincoln was elected president in 1860. Many white slaveholders in the South believed Lincoln would end slavery. Within a few weeks of his election,

SEE IT HERE!

THE CASTLE

The Smithsonian Institution Building is one of the most notable buildings on the National Mall. Built of red sandstone, it resembles a medieval castle with two ornate wings and nine towers. Today, the Castle is mainly used for offices and tourist facilities. The remains of James Smithson, who donated the money to found the Smithsonian Institution, were buried here in 1905.

WORD TO KNOW

seceded *withdrew*

South Carolina **seceded** from the Union. Other Southern states quickly followed, forming a new nation called the Confederate States of America. The conflict over slavery had torn the United States apart.

As Lincoln prepared to take office, many officials in Washington feared that Confederates might try to kill him. On Inauguration Day, federal troops marched beside Lincoln's carriage, and marksmen watched from the rooftops, ready for any sign of trouble. Lincoln mounted the inaugural platform. "I hold that . . . the Union of these States is perpetual," he told the crowd below him. "No State, upon its own mere motion, can lawfully get out of the Union."

Lincoln promised to keep the Union together. But on April 12, 1861, Confederates fired on Union troops in Fort Sumter in the harbor of Charleston, South Carolina. Three days later, Lincoln called for troops to enlist in the Union army. A divided nation plunged into civil war.

WASHINGTON AT WAR

A few days after the battle at Fort Sumter, Virginia left the Union and joined the Confederacy. Many tobacco planters in Maryland used enslaved laborers, and the state hung on the brink of secession. If Maryland left the Union, Washington would be an island surrounded by enemy forces.

In Baltimore, mobs tore up railroad tracks and cut telegraph wires. For days, Washington had almost no communication with the Northern states. Despite such actions, Maryland stayed in the Union.

From the White House, Lincoln could see the Confederate flag floating above Alexandria, Virginia, across the Potomac. The slogan, "On to Washington!" rang across the South. The capital had few defenses.

President Abraham Lincoln meets
formerly enslaved people outside the
White House, early 1860s.

Many feared that if Southern troops attacked, Confederate sympathizers in Washington would hand the city
to the enemy.

For a week, the people of Washington waited in terror.
At last, Union troops marched into the city, and tension
eased. Washington had survived the immediate crisis, but
nearly four grueling years of war still lay ahead.

In July 1861, a band of Union troops marched from
Washington to meet the Confederate army at a Virginia creek
called Bull Run. Northerners and Southerners alike believed
that the battle would bring the war to an end. Spectators
flocked after the troops, eager to watch the encounter. Like
fans at a football game, they cheered for their team to win.

Soon the spectators realized that this battle, later known as the First Battle of Bull Run (also called the First Battle of Manassas), was no game. Guns roared, and men and horses screamed in pain. Soldiers fell and died on both sides. Finally, the Confederate forces pushed the Union troops into retreat.

During the war years (1861–1865), Washington served as a major supply station for the Union army. It also became a hospital camp for wounded soldiers. Wagons loaded with injured men streamed into the city. Churches and homes turned into makeshift hospital wards, and volunteers tried their best to help the sick and wounded. Among the volunteers were the poet Walt Whitman and Louisa May Alcott, author of *Little Women*.

Confederate and Union soldiers in the First Battle of Bull Run, July 1861

To feed the hospital patients and the troops that guarded the city, army cooks turned the Capitol into a massive kitchen. They set up brick ovens in the basement and baked thousands of loaves of bread.

Lincoln appointed General George B. McClellan to head the Army of the Potomac, which would handle the city's defense. Under McClellan's command, about 200,000 Union troops guarded the capital. City streets became parade grounds as McClellan's forces went through training exercises.

On July 11, 1864, the long-dreaded attack finally came. Confederate general Jubal Early swept across the Upper Potomac and bore down on the capital. As the fighting erupted, President Lincoln watched from the wall of Fort Stevens, which had been built three years earlier to defend the capital. Suddenly, a Confederate bullet struck the soldier standing beside him. According to legend, a young army officer named Oliver Wendell Holmes shouted at the president, "Get down, you fool!" Holmes later became chief justice of the U.S. Supreme Court.

MINI-BIO

CLARA BARTON: ANGEL OF THE BATTLEFIELD

When her brother David was badly hurt in a fall, 11-year-old Clara Barton (1821–1912) nursed him night and day for nearly two years. Later, Barton taught school in Massachusetts and New Jersey. Eventually, she moved to Washington, D.C., where she worked as a clerk in the Patent Office. When the Civil War broke out, she devoted herself to rounding up food supplies and nursing the wounded. Barton's experiences during the Civil War changed her life. She saw the need for a group that would help during times of crisis. In 1881, she founded the American Red Cross, an organization that is still active today. In floods, wildfires, earthquakes, and other emergencies, Red Cross volunteers are on hand to feed the hungry and care for those left homeless.

 Want to know more? Visit www.factsfornow.scholastic.com and enter the keywords **Washington D.C.**

MINI-BIO

ELIZABETH KECKLEY: FRIEND TO THE FIRST LADY

Elizabeth Keckley (1818–1907) was born into slavery but was able to purchase her freedom. She learned to read and write, and began a dressmaking business in Washington, D.C. In 1861, the president's wife, Mary Todd Lincoln, hired her to work as a seamstress. Keckley became Mrs. Lincoln's dressmaker and personal friend and remained with her for the next seven years. As escaped slaves poured into Washington, Keckley organized a **relief** association to help them. Later, she wrote a book about her experiences.

 Want to know more? Visit www.factsfornow .scholastic.com and enter the keywords **Washington D.C.**

WORD TO KNOW

relief *financial support given to people in need*

On July 12, Early and his troops retreated. Early reported, "We didn't take Washington, but we scared Abe Lincoln." After the attempt to capture Washington failed, the tide of the war turned against the Confederacy. At last, in April 1865, Union forces marched into the Confederate capital at Richmond, Virginia. On April 9, the Confederacy surrendered.

The war years left Lincoln thin and exhausted. Yet he was determined to show the American people that life must go on. He agreed to attend a play at Washington's Ford's Theatre on the evening of April 14. As he and his wife sat in the presidential box, a supporter of the Confederacy named John Wilkes Booth crept in behind them. Suddenly, Booth raised a pistol and shot Lincoln in the back of the head. The audience screamed as they realized what had happened. Booth is reported to have shouted triumphantly in Latin, "*Sic semper tyrannis!*" ("Thus always to tyrants!"), the state motto of Virginia. As crowds stared in horror, Lincoln was carried to a house across the street. He died there early the following morning.

Lincoln's death stunned the nation. Thousands of mourners streamed into the city to pay their last respects to Lincoln, whose body lay in the Capitol Rotunda. Finally, the flag-draped coffin was loaded onto a special funeral train for the long journey to Springfield, Illinois, where the president was buried.

Crowds of people watch President Lincoln's funeral procession through the streets of Washington, D.C.

THE CHANGING CITY

The Civil War strained Washington. By the time the war ended, the city's sewage system was a threat to public health, and clean drinking water was in short supply.

The city also faced other problems. Its streets—many still unpaved—were filled with potholes. The elegant homes of the rich and powerful faced Washington's avenues. But behind those fine houses sprawled a maze of alleys lined with the shacks of the desperately poor. Many of Washington's poorest residents in the postwar years were newly freed African Americans who came to the city in search of work. Many had done farmwork all their lives, but others brought skills that prepared them to survive in the city.

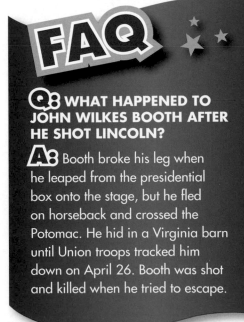

FAQ

Q: WHAT HAPPENED TO JOHN WILKES BOOTH AFTER HE SHOT LINCOLN?

A: Booth broke his leg when he leaped from the presidential box onto the stage, but he fled on horseback and crossed the Potomac. He hid in a Virginia barn until Union troops tracked him down on April 26. Booth was shot and killed when he tried to escape.

Students on the steps of a dormitory at Howard University, 1893

In 1865, Congress established the Freedmen's Bureau to educate newly freed African Americans and help them find work. The bureau opened schools for black children in the city. In 1867, it helped found Washington's Howard University, today among the country's premier Historically Black Colleges and Universities (HBCU).

Congress provided most of the money that kept Washington afloat. The city's voters elected a mayor and a 20-member council. In 1871, president Ulysses S. Grant appointed council member Alexander Shepherd to head the city's Board of Public Works. Shepherd threw himself into the task of improving the city. His crews paved streets, planted trees, installed street lamps, and dug trenches for new sewers. One of Shepherd's most ambitious projects was filling in the Washington City Canal, once part of

Tiber Creek, which had become seriously polluted. The stinking canal was replaced by Constitution Avenue.

The city's improved sanitation system, helped control Washington's epidemics of typhoid and other diseases. The work cost far more than Congress had planned to spend. In 1874, the Senate relieved Shepherd of his duties, and his programs to improve the city ground to a halt. Moreover, Congress claimed that Washington could not govern itself responsibly. Congress ended **home rule** and instead put the city under the control of three commissioners appointed by the president. The people of Washington no longer had the right to elect their own city government. The capital of the United States, the biggest democracy in the world, was being governed as if it were a colony.

FATHER OF MODERN WASHINGTON

Born in Washington, Alexander Shepherd (1835–1902) left school at age 13. He worked as a plumber's assistant and eventually worked his way up until he owned the plumbing business. Shepherd served as a member of the Washington City Council from 1861 to 1871. In 1871, he was appointed to head the city's Board of Public Works. In this position, he made many much-needed improvements. Shepherd's corrupt business practices nearly drove the city into bankruptcy, however, and he was fired. Despite these problems, he had made lasting improvements that modernized the city.

WORD TO KNOW

home rule *the right of a city, state, or nation to elect its own government*

The Library of Congress under construction in 1891

56

Snow covers the National Mall, from the Lincoln Memorial (foreground) to the Washington Monument.

1932

Veterans come to Washington demanding their bonuses

1939 ▲

Marian Anderson gives a concert at the Lincoln Memorial after being refused permission to perform at Constitution Hall

1944

Delegates from powerful nations meet in Washington to plan the United Nations

CHAPTER FIVE

MORE MODERN TIMES

★

Throughout the first three decades of the twentieth century, workers cleared trees, houses, and even a railroad station and large botanical gardens from the broad avenue leading west from the Capitol. They transformed it into the boulevard, or Mall, that Pierre-Charles L'Enfant had envisioned more than a century before.

1963
Martin Luther King Jr. delivers his "I Have a Dream" speech at the Lincoln Memorial

◄ 2009
Barack Obama is inaugurated, becoming the first African American president of the United States

2010
Congress passes the Affordable Care Act

Clerks in the U.S. Bureau of the Census, the agency that studies the nation's population, 1920s

WASHINGTON AND WORLD WAR I

In 1914, World War I engulfed Europe. Two years later, Woodrow Wilson was reelected president, campaigning on the promise that he would keep the United States out of the conflict. But Wilson came to believe that war was necessary, and the United States entered the war on April 6, 1917.

Thousands of women and men poured into Washington to take jobs in newly created "war bureaus" that filled office buildings along the Mall. Hastily built dormitories on the Grand Plaza in front of Union Station housed the flood of government workers.

Behind the closed doors of conference rooms and offices, the president and other top U.S. officials met with leaders from France, Great Britain, and the nation's other allies. They made military and political decisions that would affect the future of the world. Washington had become a center of world power in a century of many wars.

In 1918, the United States and its allies achieved victory in Europe. But when American soldiers came home, they faced many difficulties. African American veterans, who had served their country proudly, were frustrated that they still were not treated equally. Tensions flared among different ethnic groups as people competed for jobs.

The following year, tragedy struck in the United States. In 26 major cities, including Washington, white mobs rioted against black neighbors. Whites charged into black neighborhoods to destroy homes and assault people. They sometimes met armed resistance from black soldiers who had fought in World War I.

THE CHANGING FACE OF WASHINGTON

In 1921, Warren G. Harding became the first president to ride to his inauguration in an automobile instead of a horse-drawn carriage. All over the country, people were buying cars and replacing stables with garages. Cars made it easier for people who worked in Washington to live in suburban Maryland and Virginia. Cars also caused endless traffic jams on the city streets.

A car from the 1921 inaugural procession

Another change in Washington was the steady growth of the U.S. government. In 1800, the government employed only 116 people, including the president. By the 1920s, thousands of employees worked in hundreds of government offices. As departments and bureaus multiplied, they outgrew their office space. In the late 1920s, work began on a new complex of office buildings called the Federal Triangle. Buildings in the Federal Triangle include the headquarters of the U.S. Post Office, the National Archives, and the departments of Labor, Commerce, and Justice.

SEE IT HERE!

THE SUPREME
COURT BUILDING

The U.S. Supreme Court Building, which was completed in 1935, was designed to convey grandeur and dignity. It is a sparkling marble building four stories high. Above the main entrance are inscribed the words "Equal Justice Under Law." Twenty-four marble columns grace the courtroom. Throughout the building are sculptures that show scenes from the history of Western law, dating to the ancient Hebrews and Greeks.

WORD TO KNOW

stocks *shares in the ownership of a company*

Crowds gathered at the west end of the Mall in 1922 for the dedication of the Lincoln Memorial. Construction had been under way since 1912. The statue of the seated president, his head bowed in thought, came to symbolize the struggle for freedom for all people in America. But in fact, discrimination still reigned in the country, and black and white Americans were segregated at the dedication ceremony for the Lincoln Memorial.

HARD TIMES

In much of the country, the 1920s were a time of prosperity. People enjoyed the innovations that swept the country. Jazz music streamed from radios, and people packed theaters to see movies with sound.

But in 1929, the good times came to an end. The prices of **stocks** plunged, hurling the United States more deeply into the Great Depression. Across the nation, banks and factories closed, farm prices plummeted, and millions of people lost their jobs. In the District of Columbia, discouraged men in ragged clothes stood in line to get a bowl of lukewarm soup and a few slices of bread. They walked the streets searching for work, but there was none to be found.

In the spring of 1932, thousands of World War I veterans streamed into Washington. A bill passed by Congress in 1924 had guaranteed each veteran a cash bonus that would be paid in 1945. The veterans who headed to Washington supported a new bill that called for them to be paid their bonuses immediately.

By June 1932, the Bonus Army, as it came to be called, numbered about 20,000 people, of all races. Many of the veterans brought their wives and children. Some families camped in tents and shacks along Pennsylvania Avenue. The largest group set up camp on the Anacostia Flats in

Thousands of members of the Bonus Army marching on Washington in 1932

southeastern Washington. When the Senate voted against the bill to give them their bonus immediately, most of the veterans stayed on. They had served their country, and they believed that the government eventually would help them in their time of need. A journalist reported, "These were simply veterans from World War I who were out of luck, out of money, and wanted to get their bonus—and they needed the money at that moment." But General Douglas MacArthur, President Herbert Hoover's military chief of staff, feared that the Bonus Army wanted to overthrow the government.

On July 28, MacArthur ordered an assault on the Bonus Army's camp. Troops set fire to the camp. The nation was

THE BLACK CABINET

During Roosevelt's time as president, he appointed a Black Cabinet to advise him on how to improve conditions for African Americans. Members included educator Mary McLeod Bethune and Ralph Bunche, a political scientist who later received the Nobel Peace Prize for his work calming conflict in the Middle East.

horrified that the U.S. government had turned on its own citizens, especially veterans who had served their country.

THE NEW DEAL

In November 1932, voters elected a new president, Franklin D. Roosevelt. Soon after he took office, Roosevelt launched a series of programs known as the New Deal. Under these programs, people across the country built parks and libraries and schools. They brought electricity to rural areas and built dams to control flooding.

From all over the country, people poured into Washington to take jobs in newly opened offices that administered these programs. They became clerks, messengers, data collectors, and construction workers. During the years of the Great Depression, many fine buildings and monuments were constructed in the capital. Among them were the U.S. Supreme Court, the National Gallery of Art, and the Thomas Jefferson Memorial.

Singer Marian Anderson (lower left) performing on the steps of the Lincoln Memorial in 1939

But Washington continued to be segregated. Black Americans could not use the same restrooms, water fountains, and entrances as white Americans. Even members of Roosevelt's Black Cabinet were not served in the city's restaurants. In movie theaters or concert halls, black and white people had to sit in separate sections. Constitution Hall, a magnificent concert hall operated by the Daughters of the American Revolution (DAR), had a policy of hosting only white performers.

In January 1939, the DAR refused to allow the renowned African American singer Marian Anderson to sing at Constitution Hall. Despite a nationwide outcry, the DAR did not change its decision. In response, First Lady Eleanor Roosevelt and Secretary of the Interior Harold Ickes invited Anderson to give a free concert from the steps of the Lincoln Memorial. About 75,000 people gathered to hear her sing "God Bless America" and other songs. Serving as the backdrop for Anderson's concert, the Lincoln Memorial stood for the struggle of African Americans to achieve freedom and equality.

MINI-BIO

MARIAN ANDERSON: BREAKING BARRIERS WITH SONG

As a child growing up in Philadelphia, Marian Anderson (1897–1993) sang in church choirs. She decided that she wanted a career as a singer. When she applied to study at a local music school, however, she was turned away because she was African American. Anderson instead studied with a private teacher and eventually won worldwide acclaim with her stunning voice. She sang all over Europe and in New York City. In 1939, she performed for President Franklin Roosevelt and his wife, Eleanor, at the White House. When Anderson was refused permission to sing at Washington's Constitution Hall, Eleanor Roosevelt helped arrange for her to give a concert at the Lincoln Memorial. Later in her career, Anderson served as a goodwill ambassador for the United States, singing throughout the world for people of all backgrounds.

? Want to know more? Visit www.factsfornow.scholastic.com and enter the keywords **Washington D.C.**

FAQ

Q: WHAT IS THE DAR?
A: The DAR is an organization of women who can trace their ancestry back to the American Revolution.

MINI-BIO

ANNA JULIA COOPER: MAKING EDUCATION COUNT

Born into slavery and freed as a child, Anna Julia Cooper (1858–1964) grew up with a deep respect for education. She graduated from Oberlin College in Ohio and then began a long career as a teacher at Washington's all-black Dunbar High School. Under Cooper's leadership, Dunbar became one of the top high schools in the city. In 1925, she received a PhD from the University of Paris, making her the fourth African American woman to earn a doctoral degree. Throughout her long life, Cooper worked to improve education in the African American community.

? **Want to know more?** Visit www.factsfornow .scholastic.com and enter the keywords **Washington D.C.**

Though African Americans in Washington did not have full equality, the city had a thriving black middle class. African Americans owned newspapers, banks, and stores. Washington's all-black Paul Laurence Dunbar High School earned a national reputation for its academic excellence. African American families sometimes moved to the capital so their children could receive a Dunbar education. Dunbar graduates became doctors, lawyers, teachers, and political leaders at a time when few African Americans had the opportunity to enter those professions.

WORLD WAR II

World War II began in 1939 when Germany invaded Poland. Great Britain, France, and other countries joined the fight to stop Germany from taking over all of Europe. In the United States, factories and farms increased production to supply the armies of America's European allies. This increased wartime demand helped pull the nation out of the Great Depression.

At first, the United States stayed out of the war. Then, on December 7, 1941, Americans gathered around crackling radios to hear shocking news. Japanese planes had bombed the U.S. naval base at Pearl Harbor in Hawai'i. That night, a silent crowd gathered in Lafayette Square across the street from the White House, which was ablaze with lights. Behind its closed doors, the president met with diplomats, cabinet members, and generals to chart the course of the war ahead.

The capital was the center of the vast Allied war effort that defeated Japan and Germany. In the fall of 1944, as the war drew to a close, delegates from the United States, Great Britain, the **Soviet Union**, and China met at a Washington mansion called Dumbarton Oaks. They planned an international organization that would work to prevent future wars. The United Nations, which was founded in 1945, grew out of the Dumbarton Oaks Conference.

POSTWAR CHANGES

In the 1950s and 1960s, the federal government continued to grow. As office space ran short in the capital, many federal departments opened headquarters in nearby Maryland and Virginia. Many Washington residents also moved to the suburbs, buying homes in Maryland and Virginia. As more people left for the suburbs, the city's population declined from about 800,000 in 1950 to about 570,000 in 2000.

Delegates from the United States, Great Britain, the Soviet Union, and China meet at the Dumbarton Oaks Conference of 1944.

WORD TO KNOW

Soviet Union *a large nation in eastern Europe and northern and central Asia that formed in 1922 and broke apart into many different countries, including Russia, in 1991*

Teenage members of a bowling team based in a Maryland suburb of Washington, D.C., 1950s

Yet Washington, D.C., continued to attract newcomers. In the years after the war, many people from Puerto Rico and Latin America moved to Washington. Some people from Central and South America came to the capital to work in their nations' embassies, and friends and relatives joined them. A lively Latino community sprang up in the Adams-Morgan section of northeastern Washington.

"I HAVE A DREAM"

Meanwhile, life was changing for Washington's African Americans, who by 1960 made up more than half the city's population. In 1954, Washington ended its system of segregated schools. Finally, black children and white children could be educated together. Segregation, which had once been common in Washington, was disappearing.

Martin Luther King Jr., a minister from Atlanta, Georgia, was a leader in the fight to gain full citizenship rights for

African Americans. On August 28, 1963, King led more than 200,000 marchers from the Washington Monument to the Lincoln Memorial. The protest was meant to point out that although slavery had ended 100 years earlier, in some places whites still prevented African Americans from voting. African Americans still suffered discrimination, and they still needed jobs. From the steps of the Lincoln Memorial, King addressed the massive crowd: "I have a dream that one day this nation will rise up and live out the true meaning of its creed: 'We hold these truths to be self-evident, that all men are created equal.'"

Less than five years later, on the night of April 4, 1968, King was assassinated in Memphis, Tennessee. The murder of King, who had always counseled nonviolence, was a bitter blow. Fueled by rage and frustration, riots broke out in cities across the country. For three days, fires raged in Washington. More than 3,000 people were arrested, and nine people were killed before troops restored order. As Washington struggled to rebuild, city leaders pressed for a change in the way the city was governed.

Thousands of people gathered at the Martin Luther King Jr. Memorial to celebrate the 50th anniversary of King's 1963 march on Washington.

THE WATERGATE SCANDAL

On the night of June 17, 1972, a security guard caught five men breaking into Democratic National Committee Headquarters at Washington's Watergate office complex. The investigation of the Watergate scandal, as it came to be known, revealed a web of illegal activity that was intended to help President Richard Nixon's reelection campaign. Because of his involvement in the scandal, on August 9, 1974, Nixon resigned from the presidency.

WORD TO KNOW

amendment *a change to a law or legal document*

THE ROAD TO HOME RULE

In 1961, the Twenty-third **Amendment** to the Constitution granted the people of Washington, D.C., the right to vote in presidential elections. In 1964, Washingtonians could cast votes for president for the first time. Some 90 percent of the voters in the capital went to the polls. Washingtonians were still a long way from democracy, however. They had no voting representative in Congress, and they could not elect their own mayor and other city officials.

In 1970, Congress gave Washingtonians the right to elect a nonvoting member to the U.S. House of Representatives. Then in 1973, Congress passed the District of Columbia Self-Government and Reorganization Act. Under the new law, the District could elect a mayor and city council. At last, after nearly 100 years, the people of Washington were free to govern themselves. Home rule had returned to the capital.

MORE RECENT TIMES

Home rule could not solve all the city's problems. Many Washington neighborhoods were plagued by poverty and violence. City officials worked to tackle these problems.

On September 11, 2001, terrorists hijacked airplanes and crashed them into the World Trade Center in New York City and the Pentagon (the headquarters of the U.S. military) in northern Virginia. A fourth plane crashed in a field in eastern Pennsylvania. Some investigators believed that the hijackers had intended to crash the fourth plane into the Capitol. In response to the September 11 attacks, the government heightened security in the capital and throughout the nation.

Through the years, Washington, D.C., has been a place where Americans are drawn to express their views and their hopes for America. In January 2009, Washingtonians

Barack Obama takes the oath of office as president of the United States, with his wife, Michelle Obama, at his side, on January 20, 2009.

and Americans from around the country gathered for the inauguration of Barack Obama, the nation's first African American president. Forty-five years after the March on Washington, America had moved one step closer to achieving Martin Luther King Jr.'s dream.

For decades, Americans discussed the possibility of a national health care plan that would provide health insurance for all citizens. In 2010, after two years of heated congressional debate, President Barack Obama signed the Affordable Care Act into law. The goals of the act are to lower the cost of medical care and to ensure that every American has health care insurance. The major provisions of the act went into effect during 2013 and 2014.

READ ABOUT

Soccer fans cheer at a
2012 match between
the United States and
Brazil at FedEx Field
in Washington, D.C.

PEOPLE PEOPLE PEOPLE PEOPLE

CHAPTER SIX

PEOPLE

★

A SENATOR AND HIS FAMILY STROLL ALONG THE MALL, POSING FOR PHOTOGRAPHERS. A professor at Howard University gives a lecture about how the school was founded as a place to educate men and women of all races. A group of girls hurry home past a row of embassies, chatting in Spanish. All of these people and many thousands more are Washingtonians. They know firsthand the opportunities and problems of life in the nation's capital.

WHO ARE THE WASHINGTONIANS?

According to the 2010 census, Washington, D.C., is home to 601,723 people. It ranks 24th in population among cities in the United States.

Some 50 percent of all Washingtonians are African American. People of European descent make up the next-largest group in the city, accounting for about 35 percent of the population.

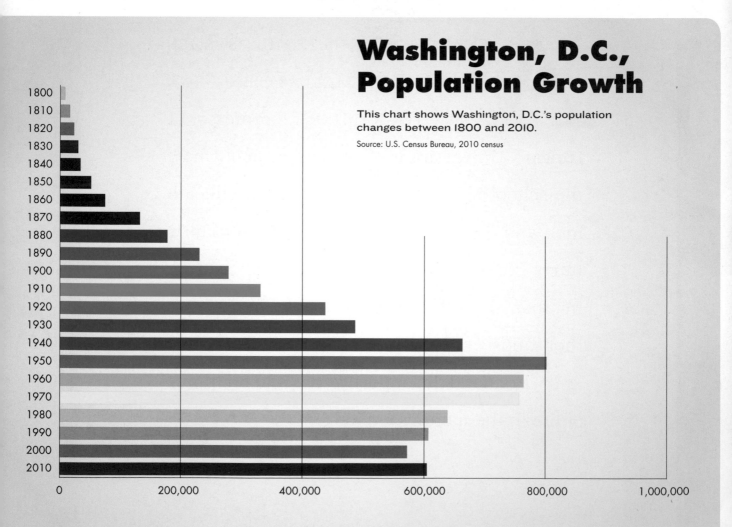

Washington, D.C., Population Growth

This chart shows Washington, D.C.'s population changes between 1800 and 2010.

Source: U.S. Census Bureau, 2010 census

A family rides their bikes near the Capitol.

People from countries all over the world live in Washington. Many immigrants work at embassies or international agencies. Others are trying to build better lives in the United States. They work in restaurants, hotels, shops, and office buildings. Some open their own businesses.

People QuickFacts

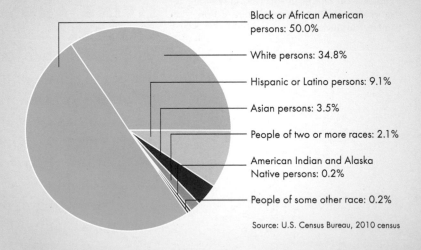

Black or African American persons: 50.0%

White persons: 34.8%

Hispanic or Latino persons: 9.1%

Asian persons: 3.5%

People of two or more races: 2.1%

American Indian and Alaska Native persons: 0.2%

People of some other race: 0.2%

Source: U.S. Census Bureau, 2010 census

ATLANTIC

Students on a school trip take a rest at the World War II Memorial, located on the National Mall.

LIVING AND WORKING IN THE CAPITAL

Wherever they go, Washingtonians are aware that they live at the center of things. Sometimes traffic is detoured for blocks to make way for a protest march. People line the sidewalks to watch the president's motorcade drive by or to greet the honored leader of a foreign nation. The city is filled with monuments, statues, and memorial squares. Students can easily take field trips to the White House, the Capitol, the Smithsonian, and other national attractions that most kids see only in books and videos.

Where Washingtonians Live

The colors on this map indicate population density throughout the district. The darker the color, the more people live there.

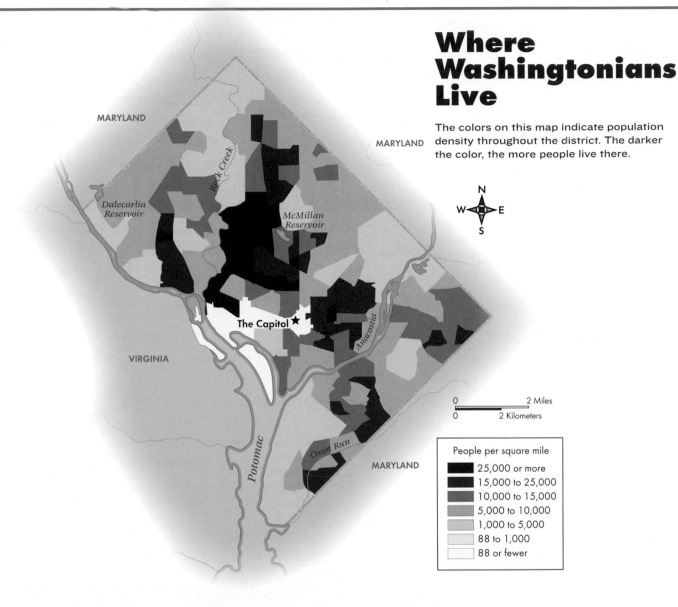

MARYLAND

MARYLAND

MARYLAND

VIRGINIA

Rock Creek

Dalecarlia Reservoir

McMillan Reservoir

Anacostia

The Capitol ★

Potomac

Oxon Run

N
W · E
S

0   2 Miles
0   2 Kilometers

People per square mile

- ■ 25,000 or more
- ■ 15,000 to 25,000
- ■ 10,000 to 15,000
- ■ 5,000 to 10,000
- ■ 1,000 to 5,000
- □ 88 to 1,000
- □ 88 or fewer

Washington's metropolitan area sprawls into Maryland suburbs such as Bethesda, Silver Spring, and College Park. It also stretches across the Potomac to embrace Alexandria, Arlington, and other cities in Virginia. Tens of thousands of people live in these cities and work in the capital. They drive or take trains and buses to and from the city. Some commuters even live in the northeastern corner of West Virginia.

HOW TO TALK LIKE A WASHINGTONIAN

When Washingtonians ride the subway, they say they are taking the Metro. The highway that loops around the city is known as the Beltway. Because of this, people often use the phrase "inside the Beltway" when talking about something related to the federal government or politics.

HOW TO EAT LIKE A WASHINGTONIAN

Lying on the cusp between the north and the south, Washington enjoys a mix of northern and southern cooking. Seafood is popular. Crabs, clams, oysters, and many varieties of fish may be fried, steamed, or baked. Southern dishes include fried chicken, grits (a cornmeal dish that is often served at breakfast), and hush puppies (a mixture of flour and cornmeal rolled into balls and deep-fried).

Washington's many immigrants bring the world's flavors to the local cuisine. At the city's restaurants and markets, among the international cuisines you can sample are Italian, Chinese, Mexican, and Middle Eastern dishes.

Shopping for fresh produce at an outdoor market in Washington, D.C.

MENU

WHAT'S ON THE MENU IN WASHINGTON, D.C.?

★ ★ ★

Senate Bean Soup

This hearty navy bean soup is on the menu every day in the restaurant of the U.S. Senate.

Maryland Crab Cakes

These fried crabmeat patties are served hot with a dash of lemon and tartar sauce.

Sweet Potato Pie

This delicious pie is filled with mashed cooked sweet potatoes blended with butter and sugar.

Hummus

Dip crackers, pita bread, or carrots in this Middle Eastern spread made from mashed chickpeas.

Pupusas

This Salvadoran snack consists of a thick tortilla filled with beans, meat, cheese, or vegetables.

TRY THIS RECIPE
Grits

This boiled cornmeal is a classic Southern breakfast dish. Have an adult nearby to help.

Ingredients:
2 cups water
1¼ cups milk
1 teaspoon salt
1 cup grits
2 tablespoons butter

Grits

Instructions:
1. Mix the water, milk, and salt in a small pot and bring to a boil.
2. Slowly pour the grits into the boiling mixture, stirring until mixed thoroughly.
3. Return the mixture to a boil, cover with a lid, and turn the heat to low. Let the mixture simmer for about 30 minutes, stirring frequently.
4. When the grits are thick and creamy, stir in the butter.
5. Remove from the heat and enjoy! Makes 4 servings.

Maryland crab cakes

Hummus and pita bread

GALLAUDET UNIVERSITY

In 1864, President Abraham Lincoln signed a bill to create a college for deaf students in northeastern Washington. Gallaudet University was named for its first president, Edward Miner Gallaudet. Most classes and lectures at Gallaudet are conducted in American Sign Language, a language based on signs made with the hands and body. Today, Gallaudet is an international center for the empowerment of deaf people and the celebration of their culture, language, and achievements.

Students near Healy Hall on the campus of Georgetown University

EDUCATION

All children in Washington are required to attend school from age 5 to age 18. The city educates some 77,000 students in its public elementary and high schools. Many more children attend private schools or are homeschooled.

Washington is home to several outstanding schools of higher education. Among them are Georgetown University and George Washington University, both of which have strong programs in international relations, and American University, which has a leading business school. Howard University, founded in 1867, is among the nation's prestigious historically black universities.

LITERARY TRADITIONS

In 1807, when Washington was little more than a muddy village, it became home to poet and philosopher Joel Barlow. Barlow lived for several years at Kalorama, an estate on Rock Creek. During his years in the capital, he wrote his epic poem *The Columbiad*, a history of Europeans in the Americas.

Historical events have inspired many writers in Washington. In 1861, a visitor from Boston, Julia Ward Howe, watched a Union regiment on the march. That night in her room at Washington's Willard Hotel, she felt inspired to write a poem. It opened with the lines, "Mine eyes have seen the glory of the coming of the Lord," and was set to a popular marching tune. Howe's "Battle Hymn of the Republic" has become one of America's enduring patriotic songs.

The Civil War also shaped the work of poet Walt Whitman, who nursed the sick and wounded in Washington's makeshift hospitals. Whitman continued to live and write in the capital until 1873. During his stay in Washington, he wrote two of his best-known poems, "O Captain! My Captain!" and "When Lilacs Last in the Dooryard Bloom'd." Both poems are tributes to President Abraham Lincoln.

Other outstanding poets who lived in Washington, D.C., include Paul Laurence Dunbar, who moved to Washington

MINI-BIO

FRANCES HODGSON BURNETT: CREATING SECRET GARDENS

When Frances Hodgson Burnett (1849–1924) was 16, her family moved from England to the United States. Burnett began writing stories to help support her widowed mother and her five younger brothers and sisters. Eventually she moved to Washington, where she continued to write. Her 1883 novel *Through One Administration* describes corruption in Washington politics. Burnett's most successful books were those she wrote for young readers. In books such as *The Secret Garden*, she wrote about lonely children who find happiness through friendship and connection with the natural world.

 Want to know more? Visit www.factsfornow .scholastic.com and enter the keywords **Washington D.C.**

Langston Hughes at his typewriter, 1940s

in 1898, and Langston Hughes, who lived in Washington in the 1920s. Their work pays tribute to the lives and struggles of working-class African Americans.

Several journalists have used their observations of Washington as the basis for novels. In 1943, Allen Drury began reporting for United Press International (UPI) on activities in the U.S. Senate. His views of the political scene led him to write a series of novels set in the capital. *Advise and Consent* won the Pulitzer Prize in 1960. Ward Just, a reporter with the *Washington Post* from 1959 to 1969, also left journalism to write fiction. Like Drury, Just set his novels against the backdrop of Washington politics and power. His books include *The Congressman Who Loved Flaubert* and *An Unfinished Season*.

STONE AND CANVAS

Washington's museums and galleries display works by the finest artists in the world. The city's public buildings are adorned with carvings and paintings, and statues and fountains grace its parks. In the early days of the republic, John Trumbull painted a series of historic panels for the Capitol Rotunda. They include *Declaration of Independence, Surrender of Lord Cornwallis,* and *General George Washington Resigning His Commission.*

Declaration of Independence
by John Trumbull

CONSTANTINO BRUMIDI: AN ARTIST WITH A MISSION

In 1852, painter Constantino Brumidi (1805–1880) fled from political turmoil in his native Italy and settled in Washington, D.C. According to one account, he declared that he wanted "to make beautiful the Capitol of the one country on earth in which there is liberty." Brumidi spent 25 years painting glorified scenes from the nation's history inside the Capitol dome. One of these paintings, *The Apotheosis of George Washington,* portrays Washington surrounded by heroic figures.

? Want to know more? Visit www.factsfornow.scholastic.com and enter the keywords **Washington D.C.**

Stone carvings on the front of the Supreme Court building

VINNIE REAM: THE YOUNGEST SCULPTOR

As a teenager during the Civil War, Vinnie Ream (1847–1914) cared for wounded soldiers in Washington's hospitals. In 1863, she began working as a sculptor, and in 1866, Congress commissioned her to carve a marble statue of President Abraham Lincoln, who had died the year before. Eighteen-year-old Ream was the first woman and the youngest artist ever to receive a commission for a statue from the U.S. government. During her career, Ream also created a monument to Admiral David Farragut and a sculpture of the Cherokee educator Sequoyah for Statuary Hall, a collection of statues in the Capitol.

? Want to know more? Visit www.factsfornow .scholastic.com and enter the keywords **Washington D.C.**

Stone carvings decorate the walls and entryways of many public buildings in the capital. Roger Morigi, an immigrant from Italy and a master stone carver, made sculptures that are now on the walls of the departments of Commerce, Justice, and Agriculture, and on the Supreme Court and the National Archives buildings. In 1956, he took the position of master carver at the Washington National Cathedral, a post he held for the next 20 years. He was deeply dedicated to his work. "[The Cathedral] may be just stone to most people," he once remarked, "but to me it's alive."

MAKING MUSIC

No matter what kind of music you like, you'll find it in Washington. The National Symphony Orchestra, founded in 1931, frequently plays at the John F. Kennedy Center Concert Hall. The Folger Shakespeare Library sponsors classical performances on replicas of historical instruments. At the Smithsonian Institution, you can hear traditional music from all over the world.

Music director Leonard Slatkin leads the National Symphony Orchestra at the John F. Kennedy Center Concert Hall in 2002.

MINI-BIO

CHUCK BROWN: GODFATHER OF GO-GO

Growing up on the streets of Washington, D.C., Chuck Brown (1936–2012) had a rough life. He quit school, performed low-level jobs, was convicted of murder, and served eight years in prison. While there, he learned to play guitar. When his sentence was up, he returned to Washington and began performing at parties with his band, the Soul Searchers. Brown's throbbing rhythms, bluesy guitar playing, and catchy lyrics soon made him a local legend in the world of funk music. He helped develop go-go, a type of dance music that mixes funk and rhythm and blues. His songs, such as "Bustin' Loose" and "We Need Some Money," provided inspiration for countless other go-go artists.

? Want to know more? Visit www.factsfor now.scholastic.com and enter the keywords **Washington D.C.**

Jazz pianist, composer, and bandleader
Duke Ellington, 1930s

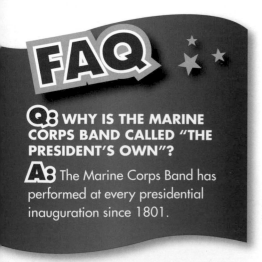

FAQ

Q8 WHY IS THE MARINE CORPS BAND CALLED "THE PRESIDENT'S OWN"?

A8 The Marine Corps Band has performed at every presidential inauguration since 1801.

In 1798, Congress established the Marine Corps Band. Nicknamed the President's Own, the Marine Corps Band is still active today. From 1880 to 1892, John Philip Sousa directed the band. Sometimes called "the March King," Sousa was a talented composer. He wrote rousing marches such as "The Washington Post" and "The Stars and Stripes Forever."

Edward Kennedy "Duke" Ellington was a different kind of bandleader. Ellington, who was born in Washington, became a celebrated jazz pianist and one of the country's greatest and most creative composers and pianists. He led a band of top jazz performers from 1923 to 1974.

GO, TEAM!

Many girls and boys in Washington love basketball. They shoot hoops in parks, back alleys, and school gyms. Under coach John Thompson, Georgetown University developed a powerhouse team in the 1980s. Center Patrick Ewing led the team to a national championship in 1984.

Fans of pro basketball cheer on the Washington Wizards, and hockey lovers follow the Washington Capitals. Football fans root for the Washington Redskins, who play in Landover, Maryland. Until 1971, the capital had a professional baseball team called the Washington Senators. Over its long history, the team produced many great players, including Hall of Fame pitcher Walter Johnson and first baseman Mickey Vernon. Major League Baseball returned to Washington in 2005, when the Washington Nationals began playing in the city.

Darrell Young of the Washington Redskins runs the ball in a 2013 game against the Dallas Cowboys.

READ ABOUT

A school group at the
Lincoln Memorial

CHAPTER SEVEN

GOVERNMENT

★

AS THE U.S. CAPITAL, WASHINGTON HAS A UNIQUE RELATIONSHIP WITH THE NATION'S FEDERAL GOVERNMENT. The city elects its own mayor and city council members, but the federal government must approve the laws the city government passes. Although Washington, D.C., stands as a symbol of democracy, its elected officials do not always have final say about how their city is run.

CAPITOL FACTS

Here are some fascinating facts about the U.S. Capitol.

- The U.S. Capitol in Washington has five stories and stands 288 feet (88 m) high from the floor of the Rotunda to the top of the dome.
- The Capitol sits on 274 acres (111 ha) of grounds that were designed by landscape architect Frederick Law Olmsted, who also designed New York City's Central Park.
- American flags have flown day and night on the east and west sides of the Capitol dome since World War I. Flags also fly on the north and south sides of the dome when Congress is in session.
- The Capitol's National Statuary Hall contains 100 statues, two donated by each state. The last to be erected was the statue of Pueblo Indian leader Popay, contributed by New Mexico in 2005.
- In the early 1800s, the Capitol contained a room of baths for senators and guests. Today, two marble bathtubs from this room are stored in the basement.

The U.S. Capitol

POWER TO THE PEOPLE

In 1973, Congress granted home rule to the people of Washington, D.C. Today, Washington voters elect a mayor and a 13-member city council. Five members of the council are elected by the city as a whole, and each of the city's eight districts, called wards, chooses one more member. So, a Washingtonian can vote for six candidates for the city council. The council passes bills about traffic, schools, sanitation, street repairs, and other aspects of city life.

SEE IT HERE!

THE JOHN A. WILSON BUILDING

The mayor's office and other city departments are housed in the John A. Wilson Building, Washington's city hall. The Wilson Building, named for a leader of the home rule movement in the 1970s and a former chairperson of the Washington City Council, is a six-story marble structure in the Federal Triangle north of the National Mall. Bronze plaques in the lobby honor the men and women who have served as commissioners during Washington's history.

The National Mall

This map shows places of interest on the National Mall (shown in green) in Washington, D.C.

MINI-BIO

EDWARD W. BROOKE III: SPEAKING FROM THE SENATE

Edward W. Brooke III (1919–) grew up in Washington and graduated from Howard University. After serving in World War II, he earned a law degree at Boston University. In 1962, Brooke was elected to serve as attorney general in Massachusetts. When he was elected to the U.S. Senate in 1967, he became the first African American senator since 1881. As a senator, Brooke worked to promote civil rights and provide better housing for the poor.

Want to know more? Visit www.factsfornow.scholastic.com and enter the keywords **Washington D.C.**

Washington, D.C.'s police officers enforce laws and keep peace in the city.

The mayor of Washington approves bills that are passed by the city council to make them law or vetoes them to reject them. He or she appoints the heads of city departments such as the police department, the health department, and the transportation department, and picks four people to serve on the Board of Education.

THE COURTS

Washington's judicial branch of government consists of two courts. Most trials take place in the Superior Court of

Washington, D.C., Quadrants

This map shows the four quadrants of Washington, D.C., and their neighborhoods.

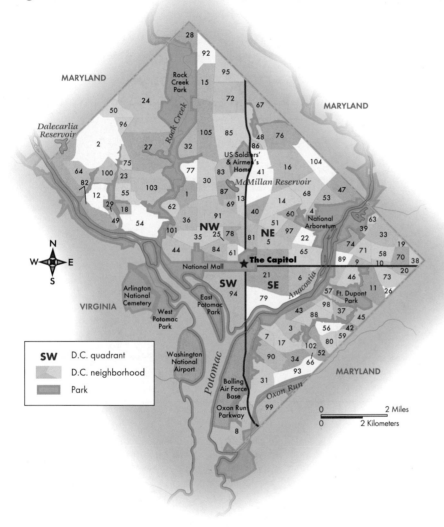

the District of Columbia. The Superior Court is made up of several divisions that handle different types of cases such as criminal cases, family issues, and tax cases. The D.C. Court of Appeals is the highest court in the city. Its nine justices review decisions made in the Superior Court.

Representing Washington, D.C.

This list shows the number of elected officials who represent Washington, D.C.

OFFICE	LENGTH OF TERM
Mayor	4 years
City Council	2 years

TAXATION WITHOUT REPRESENTATION

Although Washingtonians vote for their own city leaders, federal authorities still have a strong hand in city government. Congress reviews every law passed by the city council and approved by the mayor. District laws and the city's budget are not finalized until they win the approval of Congress and the president.

District Government

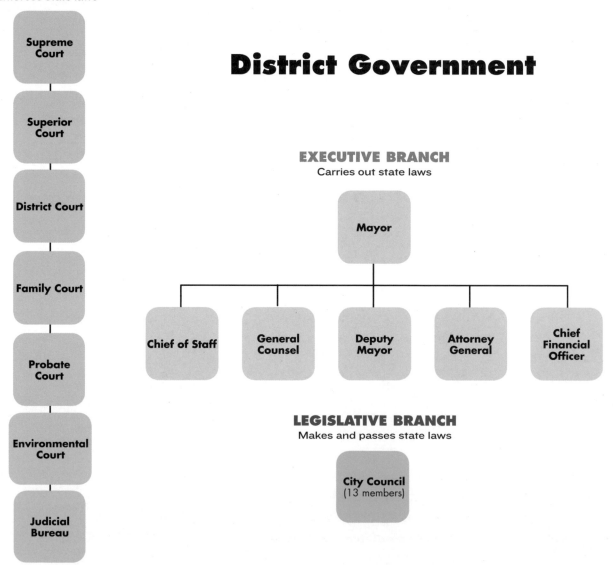

JUDICIAL BRANCH
Enforces state laws

- Supreme Court
- Superior Court
- District Court
- Family Court
- Probate Court
- Environmental Court
- Judicial Bureau

EXECUTIVE BRANCH
Carries out state laws

Mayor

- Chief of Staff
- General Counsel
- Deputy Mayor
- Attorney General
- Chief Financial Officer

LEGISLATIVE BRANCH
Makes and passes state laws

City Council
(13 members)

The people of Washington elect one representative to Congress. The representative from the District can serve on committees but cannot vote on bills. Nevertheless, D.C. residents pay all federal taxes and are subject to all federal laws.

MINI-BIO

ELEANOR HOLMES NORTON: SPEAKING FOR WASHINGTON

Eleanor Holmes Norton (1937–) grew up in Washington, D.C. In college and at Yale Law School, she became active in the civil rights movement. She later became a law professor and worked in the government trying to end discrimination against women. In 1990, Norton was elected Washington, D.C.'s representative to the U.S. Congress. Throughout her career, she has been a strong supporter of full representation for the people of the District.

? **Want to know more?** Visit www.factsfornow.scholastic.com and enter the keywords **Washington D.C.**

THINK ABOUT IT!

Fighting for Rights

In November 2000, the District of Columbia issued license plates with a new slogan: "Taxation Without Representation." The slogan refers to the fact that D.C. residents pay federal income taxes yet have no voting representative in Congress. "We want our rights now," said Washington's nonvoting representative Eleanor Holmes Norton. "We can compel Congress to give us full representation." She suggested that D.C. residents should be exempt from paying taxes until they have a representative who can vote on their behalf.

Q: **BESIDES THE REPRESENTATIVE FROM WASHINGTON, D.C., ARE THERE ANY OTHER NONVOTING MEMBERS OF CONGRESS?**

A: Puerto Rico, Guam, American Samoa, the Northern Mariana Islands, and the U.S. Virgin Islands all elect members to Congress who cannot vote on bills.

District Flag

The Washington, D.C., flag is based on the shield from George Washington's family coat of arms. The flag, adopted in 1938, consists of three red stars above two horizontal red bars on a white background.

District Seal

The seal shows a woman representing justice hanging a wreath on a statue of George Washington. In the background are the U.S. Capitol and a train steaming in front of a rising sun. The words "District of Columbia" run across the top of the seal, and the motto *Justitia Omnibus*, Latin for "Justice for All," is in a banner at the bottom. Just above this banner is the date 1871, the year the seal was adopted.

A worker oversees the printing of money at the U.S. Bureau of Engraving and Printing.

CHAPTER EIGHT

ECONOMY

★

IN SOME U.S. TOWNS, ONE COMPANY DOMINATES THE LOCAL ECONOMY BECAUSE MOST OF THE RESIDENTS WORK FOR THAT COMPANY. These places are known as company towns. Washington, D.C., has sometimes been called "the nation's biggest company town" because so many of its workers are employed by one vast "company": the United States government.

A member of the Capitol Hill Police on bicycle patrol

More than 200,000 people in the Washington area work for the U.S. government.

WORKING FOR THE FEDS

Most U.S. cities developed as centers of trade and manufacturing. But manufacturing and trade have never been part of Washington's economy. Since the city was founded, the federal government has been the basis of its economy.

Some government workers, such as senators, cabinet members, and the president, are known throughout the world. Thousands of others work behind the scenes to keep operations running smoothly. They clean offices, program computers, and run errands. Some conduct research, some file records, and others write government reports. People who work for government agencies such as the Internal Revenue Service (IRS) and Social

Security Administration—which have headquarters in Washington—are all federal employees. Washingtonians sometimes say as shorthand that they work for the "Feds."

MILLIONS OF VISITORS

Tourism is also important to Washington's economy. The nation's capital is a magnet for people of all ages and backgrounds. They come to see monuments, visit museums, and walk the historic streets. Each year, about 19 million visitors stream through the city—almost 32 times the number of people who actually live there!

What Do Washingtonians Do?

This color-coded chart shows what industries Washingtonians work in.

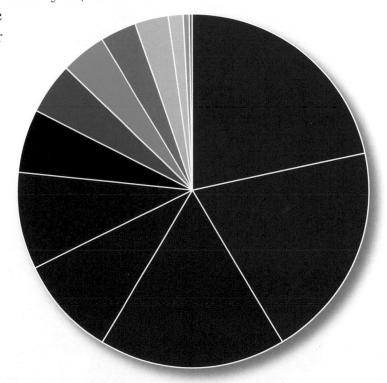

21.8% Professional, scientific, and management, and administrative and waste management services 67,188

19.7% Educational services, and health care and social assistance 60,707

17.2% Public administration 53,164

9.3% Arts, entertainment, and recreation, and accommodation and food services 28,665

9.0% Other services, except public administration 27,703

5.7% Finance and insurance, and real estate and rental and leasing 17,575

4.8% Retail trade 14,869

4.2% Information 12,905

3.3% Transportation and warehousing, and utilities 10,139

3.1% Construction 9,478

1.3% Manufacturing 3,929

0.6% Wholesale trade 1,932

0.1% Agriculture, forestry, fishing and hunting, and mining 348

Source: U.S. Census Bureau, 2010 census

SEE IT HERE!

THE METRO

Washington's subway system, called the Metro, is the second-busiest rapid transit system in the United States (behind New York City's). Clean, comfortable trains whisk passengers along 106 miles (171 km) of track through Washington and its suburbs. The system includes 86 stations along five linked train lines. Construction on the Metro began in 1969, and the first section opened in 1976.

Tourists need places to eat and sleep. They take taxis, ride the Metro, buy newspapers, attend movies, and find dozens of other ways to spend their money in the nation's capital. A big tourist year is good news for Washington businesses.

BEYOND GOVERNMENT AND TOURISM

Many Washingtonians work at dozens of national and international organizations that have their headquarters in Washington. These include the National Geographic Society and the American Red Cross. Organizations often choose to be based in Washington for easy access to mem-

A concierge at the Willard Hotel assists a hotel guest on the phone.

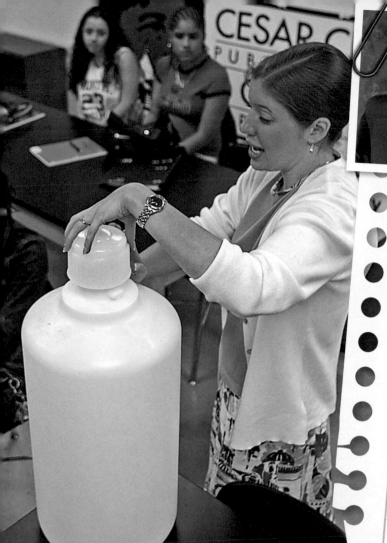

MINI-BIO

KATHARINE GRAHAM: WOMAN OF THE PRESS

In the early 1960s, few women ran large businesses. When Katharine Graham (1917–2001) took over as publisher and board chair of the Washington Post, she was the first woman in the nation to head one of the country's 500 largest companies. Under Graham's leadership, reporters Bob Woodward and Carl Bernstein broke the story about the Watergate scandal. Through the paper, Graham worked to support health care, day care facilities, and the arts in Washington. Her memoir, *Personal History*, won the Pulitzer Prize in 1998.

? **Want to know more?** Visit www.factsfor now.scholastic.com and enter the keywords **Washington D.C.**

A teacher explains a science concept to students at one of the César Chávez Public Charter Schools.

bers of Congress and other government officials. They lobby members of Congress to support legislation they favor.

Like any city, Washington has many businesses and services to meet the needs of its residents. Schools and hospitals, stores, newspapers, gas stations, and beauty salons all play their part in the city's economy.

FAQ

Q8 WHERE DOES THE TERM *LOBBY* COME FROM?

A8 During the 19th century, people representing companies or organizations used to approach congresspeople in the lobbies of buildings to talk about their concerns. Today, "to lobby" means to talk to a member of Congress in an attempt to persuade him or her to vote for or against a particular bill.

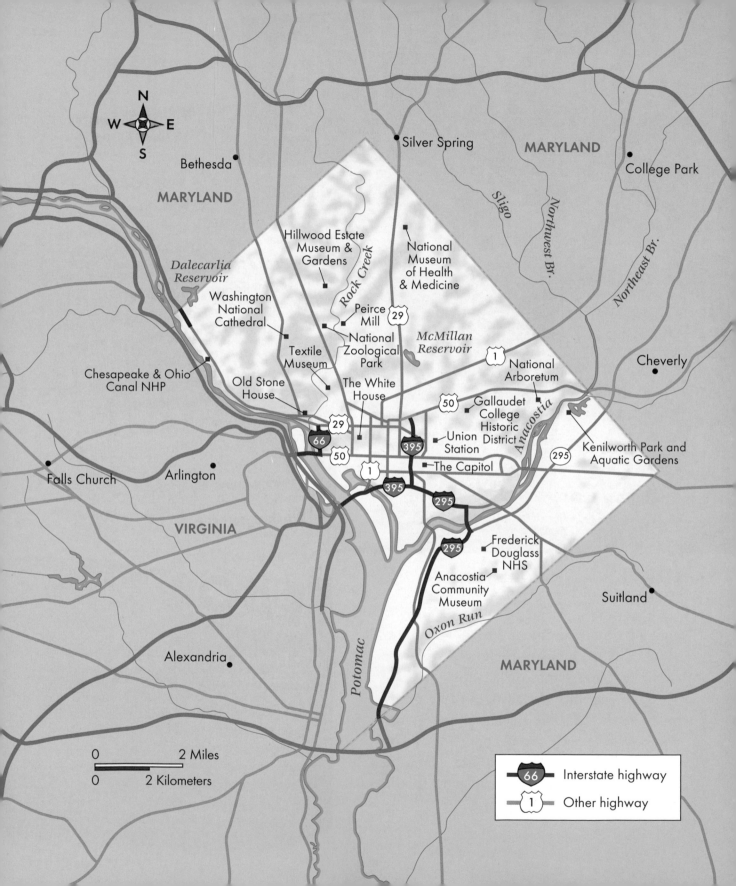

N
W · E
S

Bethesda

MARYLAND

Silver Spring

MARYLAND

College Park

Dalecarlia Reservoir

Hillwood Estate Museum & Gardens

National Museum of Health & Medicine

Sligo

Northwest Br.

Northeast Br.

Washington National Cathedral

Rock Creek

Peirce Mill

29

McMillan Reservoir

Cheverly

Textile Museum

National Zoological Park

1

National Arboretum

Anacostia

Chesapeake & Ohio Canal NHP

Old Stone House

The White House

50

Gallaudet College Historic District

Kenilworth Park and Aquatic Gardens

29

66

50

Union Station

395

295

Falls Church

Arlington

1

The Capitol

VIRGINIA

395

295

Alexandria

295

Frederick Douglass NHS

Suitland

Anacostia Community Museum

Oxon Run

MARYLAND

Potomac

0   2 Miles
0   2 Kilometers

66   Interstate highway

1   Other highway

CHAPTER NINE

TRAVEL GUIDE

★

WITH ITS GRAND MONUMENTS AND MAGNIFICENT MUSEUMS, WASHINGTON, D.C., PROVIDES VISITORS WITH MANY DAZZLING ATTRACTIONS. The city is also home to dozens of lesser known museums, statues, and landmarks that you won't want to miss. Walk the streets, explore the parks, marvel at the exhibits, and watch the people all around you.

← Follow along with this travel map. We'll see all the sights around the nation's capital.

CAPITOL HILL AND THE FEDERAL TRIANGLE

THINGS TO DO: Attend a session of Congress, view the original Declaration of Independence at the National Archives, or read a news story on camera at a journalism museum.

★ **United States Botanic Garden:**
See flowers, shrubs, and trees from all over the world at these carefully landscaped gardens at the southwest edge of the Capitol grounds. About 10,000 varieties of plants are on display.

SEE IT HERE!

THE U.S. CAPITOL

Construction began on the U.S. Capitol in 1793 and continued on and off for decades. Congress first began meeting in the Capitol in 1800, long before it was complete. Today, the public is welcome to watch Congress in action. The U.S. Capitol is not only the seat of Congress, it is also a fine place to see works of art. Paintings by Constantino Brumidi line the Senate wing, or Brumidi Corridors, and new works have been added to commemorate the 1969 moon landing and other great moments in U.S. history. The Capitol grounds include sweeping lawns, quiet walkways, gardens, and fountains.

★ **Library of Congress:** The Library of Congress was created in 1800 as a research library for members of the House and Senate. Today, the library holds about 100 million items, including books, magazines, newspapers, films, audio recordings, and historic photographs.

★ **Capitol Hill Visitor Center:** Located underground on the east side of the Capitol Building, this exhibition hall features artifacts, photographs, and films that tell the history of Congress and the Capitol.

The Library of Congress contains more books than any other library in the world.

The Main Reading Room of the Thomas Jefferson Building at the Library of Congress

★ **Folger Shakespeare Library:** Next to the Library of Congress is the Folger Shakespeare Library, which is dedicated to work by and about William Shakespeare.

★ **The National Archives and Records Administration:** Housing about 3 billion records related to the United States and its government, this building is nicknamed the Nation's Filing Cabinet. On display in the Rotunda are the original Declaration of Independence, the U.S. Constitution, and the **Bill of Rights**. The National Archives hosts rotating exhibits based on items in its vast collection.

WORD TO KNOW

Bill of Rights *a document listing the first ten amendments, or changes, to the U.S. Constitution*

In the event of an emergency, the Declaration of Independence, the Constitution, and the Bill of Rights will automatically descend into an underground vault for safekeeping.

Visitors at the Newseum

★ **Newseum:** This museum celebrates every aspect of news reporting. It displays items from some of the biggest stories in recent history, such as a copy of the world's first Web page (created in 1992) and a door taped open by the men who broke into the Watergate office complex in 1972, a crime that eventually led to President Richard Nixon's resignation. You can browse hundreds of historic newspapers or try your hand at reading a TV news script on camera.

NORTHWEST WASHINGTON

THINGS TO DO: Search for the oldest tombstone in Oak Hill Cemetery, tour the White House, or crack a code at the International Spy Museum.

★ **Peirce Mill:** Until 1958, this water-powered mill on Rock Creek ground grain for use by government cafeterias. Today, visitors can see old wooden mill gears and massive millstones dating to the 1820s.

★ **Chesapeake and Ohio Canal National Historical Park:** In 1825, the canal opened, linking Chesapeake Bay and the Ohio River. The canal ceased operation in 1924, but you can still see its carefully preserved locks and dams.

White House, south portico and south lawn

★ **Old Stone House:** Built in 1765, the Old Stone House is the oldest surviving building in Washington. The house is furnished to look much as it did during the American Revolution.

★ **Oak Hill Cemetery:** This cemetery, which dates to 1848, contains the graves of many notable Washingtonians.

★ **Ford's Theatre:** For more than a century after the assassination of Abraham Lincoln, Ford's Theatre was closed. In 1968, it reopened as both a theater and a historic site.

★ **The White House:** The outside of the White House looks much as it did when it was completed in 1800, although the interior has undergone many renovations. Visitors can tour several rooms in the historic home.

★ **LeDroit Park:** This cozy neighborhood is home to sprawling Victorian mansions, handsome row houses, and a large community garden. The area, once a major community of wealthy African Americans, today features a diverse mix of ethnic groups.

★ **African American Civil War Museum:** This museum presents photographs, newspapers, clothing, uniforms, and weaponry of the Civil War era in commemoration of the 200,000 black troops that served in the conflict.

Corcoran Gallery of Art

★ **Corcoran Gallery of Art:** This renowned art museum has a collection that includes works by American masters, such as Winslow Homer, John Singer Sargent, and Augustus Saint-Gaudens.

★ **Washington National Cathedral:** Constructed from 1907 to 1990, this is the second-largest **gothic** cathedral in the country (behind New York City's Cathedral Church of St. John the Divine).

WORD TO KNOW

gothic *a style of architecture that features pointed arches*

★ **National Portrait Gallery:** This museum displays portraits of people who have been influential in U.S. and world history. Paintings and photographs show ordinary people as well as the rich and powerful. The faces of presidents, actors, teachers, and farmhands are preserved here for future generations.

★ **National Building Museum:** In this museum, you can view exhibits on all aspects of architecture and the preservation of historic buildings. The permanent exhibit *Washington: Symbol and City* covers the construction of the nation's capital.

★ **National Museum of Health and Medicine:** A Civil War hospital occupied this building in 1862. Today, the museum preserves the history of military medicine and explores changing ideas about anatomy and the treatment of disease through American history. Collections include antique surgical instruments, early X-ray equipment, and historic medical books and drawings. If you think you'd like to study medicine someday, try cutting open a simulated dead body in an interactive exhibit.

★ **International Spy Museum:** Hidden microphones, secret cameras, coded messages—explore a world of intrigue in this fascinating museum. Learn about important spies and try to read a coded message.

★ **Old Post Office Tower:** The post office moved out of this building in 1934, and today it houses federal offices. The clock tower contains exhibits on the history of the building, and from the top you get a spectacular view.

★ **National Postal Museum:** Trace the history of mail delivery from colonial times to the present at this unique museum. On display are historic letters and postcards, greeting cards through the centuries, and a vast collection of postage stamps.

★ **National Museum of Women in the Arts:** This museum honors the contributions of female painters, sculptors, architects, musicians, singers, dancers, and filmmakers. Their stories are told through photos, videos, letters, newspaper clippings, and recorded interviews, and galleries overflow with examples of their work.

Pandas at the National Zoo

★ **National Zoo:** The zoo is home to birds, mammals, and reptiles representing 400 species. The African Savanna and Amazon rain forest exhibits allow visitors to watch animals in their natural habitats. The zoo has a highly successful breeding program with endangered species, particularly the giant panda.

★ **Hillwood Estate, Museum & Gardens:** Overlooking Rock Creek, this mansion was once owned by a member of the family that founded Post Cereals. Today, the house is a museum of Russian art. The landscaped grounds include a rose garden, a Japanese garden, and several greenhouses.

★ **Textile Museum:** Turkish carpets, Peruvian blankets, and Chinese silk cloth are all on display at this museum. Exhibits show how fabrics are woven and explore the history of the textile industry.

NORTHEAST WASHINGTON

THINGS TO DO: See water lilies at an aquatic garden, browse the shops at Union Station, or take a tram ride through the National Arboretum.

★ **Kenilworth Park and Aquatic Gardens:** This unusual garden boasts dozens of varieties of water lilies, lotuses, and other water plants. In 1938, the gardens became part of the national park system.

★ **Sewall-Belmont House and Museum:** Built in 1800, this house has been the headquarters of the National Woman's Party since 1929. The museum displays statues and portraits of early **suffragists** as well as the desk of suffragist leader Susan B. Anthony.

WORD TO KNOW

suffragists *people who campaigned for women's right to vote.*

Inside Union Station

★ **Union Station:** Constructed of marble, granite, and gold leaf, this magnificent building has long been a symbol of the nation's capital. The station fell into disuse after World War II, but it was revived as an indoor mall in 1988 with shops, restaurants, and movie theaters. At the back of the station, trains still roll in and out day and night, linking Washington with the rest of the country.

★ **Gallaudet College Historic District:** A number of fine examples of late 19th-century architecture are preserved on the campus of Gallaudet University. The school's outstanding buildings include Chapel Hall and College Hall.

NATIONAL WOMAN'S PARTY

Founded by suffragists Alice Paul and Lucy Burns in 1917, the National Woman's Party (NWP) worked for 80 years to secure equal rights for women. It never ran a candidate for office. Instead, it promoted laws that would give women equality with men in employment, education, and the political process. Today, the NWP focuses on preserving the history of the women's rights movement.

★ **U.S. National Arboretum:** Ride a tram through this 446-acre (180 ha) park planted with trees and shrubs from all over the world. The arboretum has areas devoted to Asian trees, conifers (cone-bearing trees), and miniature Japanese trees. Scientists at the arboretum conduct research on tree diseases, trees that can flourish in cities, and much more.

A path in the U.S. National Arboretum

ON THE MALL

THINGS TO DO: See a rock from the moon, read Lincoln's stirring words at the Lincoln Memorial, and honor fallen soldiers at the Vietnam Veterans Memorial.

★ **The National Mall:** This area stretches from the Capitol to the Lincoln Memorial and includes many parks and a large reflecting pool.
★ **Arthur M. Sackler Gallery:** The Sackler is one of two museums in the Smithsonian Institution that feature the art of East and South Asia.
★ **Freer Gallery of Art:** Connected by tunnels to the Sackler, the Freer Gallery also exhibits Asian art. On display are Chinese ceramics, folding Japanese screens, and wood carvings from Thailand.
★ **National Museum of African Art:** Established in 1964 as a private museum, this collection became part of the Smithsonian in 1979. It includes exhibits about the arts and crafts of Africa's many cultures, past and present.

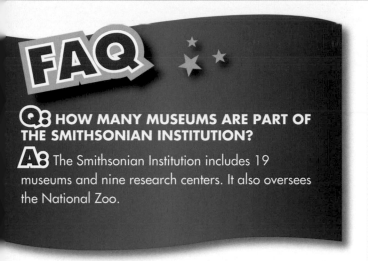

FAQ

Q8 HOW MANY MUSEUMS ARE PART OF THE SMITHSONIAN INSTITUTION?

A8 The Smithsonian Institution includes 19 museums and nine research centers. It also oversees the National Zoo.

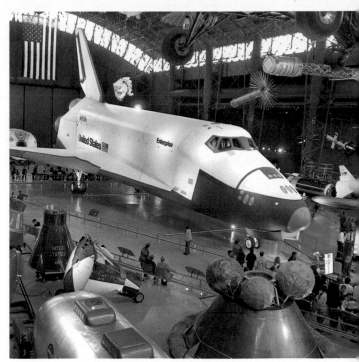

National Air and Space Museum

★ **National Air and Space Museum:** Here you'll find the world's largest collection of planes and spacecraft. On display are historic crafts such as the *Spirit of St. Louis,* the plane in which Charles Lindbergh made the world's first solo flight across the Atlantic in 1927, and the command module of *Apollo 11*, which in 1969 became the first spacecraft to carry humans to the moon. The museum even includes a real piece of moon rock! Among the other items in the museum are the original plane flown by the Wright brothers in 1903, and the filming model of the Starship *Enterprise* that carried Captain Kirk, Mr. Spock, and their friends through several seasons of *Star Trek.*

★ **National Museum of Natural History:** Plants, animals, fossils, minerals, and human artifacts are all on display here in astounding abundance. One of the most popular attractions is the 45-carat Hope Diamond. The Hall of Dinosaurs displays skeletons, eggs, and footprints of the long-gone giants, and the Hall of Mammals contains stuffed specimens in lifelike surroundings.

★ **National Gallery of Art:** This museum holds an extraordinary collection of work by American and European artists.

★ **National Museum of the American Indian:** Members of several Native American groups advised and planned the construction of this museum, which opened in 2004. The building is made of natural stone and has gentle curves rather than sharp angles. Inside are displays of Pueblo and Navajo pottery, Lakota war bonnets, totem poles from Alaska, Iroquois bows and arrows, and much more. The museum sponsors many programs, including traditional music and dance.

★ **Hirshhorn Museum and Sculpture Garden:** The Hirshhorn is one of the most unusual buildings on the Mall. It looks a bit like a spaceship—a large cylinder supported by four legs. Inside are paintings and sculptures by the greatest artists of the 20th century. Its sculpture garden features works by artists such as Auguste Rodin and Alexander Calder.

PRESERVING HER HERITAGE

When she was growing up in New York City, Gabrielle Tayac (1967–) was very aware of her Piscataway roots. Her grandfather, Turkey Tayac, was a notable Piscataway leader and the last person who knew the Piscataway language. Gabrielle Tayac earned a doctorate from Harvard University and later settled in Maryland, where she threw herself into research on Piscataway history and culture. She was thrilled to find a pile of slips of paper on which her grandfather had written Piscataway words and their English meanings. Tayac is now a historian at the Smithsonian Institution's National Museum of the American Indian, trying to preserve and revive the traditions of Native Americans across the country.

Hirshhorn Museum sculpture garden

★ **National World War II Memorial:** This monument honors those Americans who served in the armed forces during World War II and those who aided in the war effort from the home front. The monument consists of 56 pillars arranged in a semicircle around a plaza. Facing each other across the plaza are two stately 43-foot (13 m) arches. The stories of the war and the home front are told in 24 bronze sculptures.

★ **U.S. Holocaust Memorial Museum:** This museum explores the history of the Holocaust during World War II. The stories of those who died and those who survived are told through pictures, letters, diaries, and artifacts such as clothes and toys. The museum also explores more recent **genocides**, such as the killings in Rwanda, Africa.

WORD TO KNOW

genocides *systematic destructions of national, racial, political, or cultural groups*

★ **National Museum of American History:** This museum includes exhibits such as *America on the Move*, which traces the history of transportation in the United States from 1876 to the present. Other popular displays include props from famous TV shows, the inaugural gowns of the first ladies, and presidential memorabilia such as George Washington's uniform and Bill Clinton's saxophone.

★ **Lincoln Memorial:** One of the most beloved monuments in the capital, the Lincoln Memorial consists of three chambers surrounded by 38 columns. The walls of the north chamber are inscribed with words from Lincoln's Second Inaugural Address. His Gettysburg Address is inscribed in the south chamber. In the central hall is a seated figure of Lincoln, his head bowed in thought. The statue is 19 feet (6 m) tall.

Lincoln Memorial

★ **Korean War Veterans Memorial:**
The grueling drudgery of war comes
to life in this monument to the
people who fought in the Korean
War. The statues depict 19 men,
each rendered in careful detail,
trudging out from the trees and up
a hill. Weighed down with their gear
and weapons, they look tired but
determined to move forward. This
monument was dedicated in 1995 to
the men of a conflict that is sometimes called the Forgotten War.

★ **Vietnam Veterans Memorial:** This
memorial was designed by a
21-year-old college student named
Maya Ying Lin. It consists of a black,
reflective V-shaped wall inscribed
with the names of the more than
58,000 American men and women
who died in the Vietnam War.

Vietnam Veterans Memorial

SOUTH OF THE MALL

**THINGS TO DO: Shop at the
Eastern Market, learn about
African American history at the Anacostia
Community Museum, and climb to the top of the
Washington Monument.**

★ **Eastern Market:** Built after the Civil
War, this market is the place to buy
local fruits and vegetables, seafood,
meat, cheese, baked goods, crafts, and
much more.

★ **Anacostia Community Museum:**
This museum has an outstanding
collection of maps, letters, newspapers, and photos that explore the
lives of African Americans from
colonial times to the present.

★ **Franklin Delano Roosevelt
Memorial:** This monument to
Franklin Delano Roosevelt consists of four rooms, one for each
of the president's terms in office.
Sculptures within each room tell
the story of Roosevelt's life and of
the nation as it weathered the Great
Depression and World War II.

★ **Martin Luther King, Jr.
Memorial:** This memorial to the
great civil rights leader was opened
in 2011, on the 48th anniversary of
the historic March on Washington.

★ **Frederick Douglass National Historic Site:** The abolitionist and writer Frederick Douglass lived in this house, also called Cedar Hill, from 1877 to 1895. When Douglass bought the home, African Americans were not allowed to buy homes in the neighborhood, but he defied that rule.

MINI-BIO

FREDERICK DOUGLASS: FIGHTER FOR FREEDOM

Growing up enslaved in eastern Maryland, Frederick Douglass (1817–1895) realized that reading was the key to freedom. He taught himself to read and eventually escaped from slavery. In 1841, he began to speak in the North against slavery, and he became a stirring spokesman for abolition. After the Civil War, he worked for women's rights. He lived in Washington from 1877 until his death. During this time, he served the government as Recorder of Deeds of the District of Columbia and as the U.S. minister to Haiti.

? **Want to know more?** Visit www.factsfor now.scholastic.com and enter the keywords **Washington D.C.**

★ **Thomas Jefferson Memorial:** This memorial consists of a 19-foot (6 m) statue of Thomas Jefferson standing within a circle of columns beneath a dome. Words from the Declaration of Independence and other writings by Jefferson are inscribed within the memorial. In the spring, delicate pink and white blossoms adorn the cherry trees that surround the memorial.

SEE IT HERE!

WASHINGTON MONUMENT

Pierre-Charles L'Enfant dreamed that a magnificent monument to George Washington would rise in the capital city. The Washington Monument, built between 1848 and 1885, is a soaring spire of white marble that rises 555 feet (169 m) high, making it the tallest structure in the city. The monument is crowned by an observation platform. From there, you can gaze over the grand city that Washington has become.

 A winding flight of 897 steps rises to the top of the Washington Monument.

WRITING PROJECTS

Check out these ideas for creating a campaign brochure and writing you-are-there narratives. Or research the lives of famous people from Washington, D.C.

118

ART PROJECTS

You can illustrate the state song, create a dazzling PowerPoint presentation, or learn about the district quarter and design your own.

119

TIMELINE

What happened when? This timeline highlights important events in the district's history—and shows what was happening throughout the United States at the same time.

122

GLOSSARY

Remember the Words to Know from the chapters in this book? They're all collected here.

125

FAST FACTS

Use this section to find fascinating facts about symbols, land area and population statistics, weather, sports teams, and much more.

126

SCIENCE, TECHNOLOGY, ENGINEERING, & MATH PROJECTS

120

Make weather maps, graph population statistics, and research endangered species that live in the state.

PRIMARY VS. SECONDARY SOURCES

121

So what are primary and secondary sources? And what's the diff? This section explains all that and where you can find them.

BIOGRAPHICAL DICTIONARY

133

This at-a-glance guide highlights some of the district's most important and influential people. Visit this section and read about their contributions to the region, the country, and the world.

RESOURCES

Books and much more. Take a look at these additional sources for information about the state.

138

WRITING PROJECTS

Write a Memoir, Journal, or Editorial for Your School Newspaper!

Picture Yourself . . .

★ Moving to Washington in early 1800s. What does the city look like? What is life like for the people who live there?
SEE: Chapter Four, pages 44–45.

★ Taking part in the 1963 March on Washington. Write a story for your school newspaper discussing the march. Describe the sights and sounds of being in a crowd of more than 200,000 people on the Mall in front of the Lincoln Memorial. Explain how you felt when Martin Luther King Jr. began talking. How did the people around you react?
SEE: Chapter Five, page 67.

Create an Election Brochure or Web Site!

Run for office! Throughout this book, you've read about some of the issues that concern Washington, D.C., today. As a candidate for mayor of Washington, D.C., create a campaign brochure or Web site.

★ Explain how you meet the qualifications to be mayor of Washington, D.C.

★ Talk about the three or four major issues you'll focus on if you're elected.

★ Remember, you'll be responsible for Washington, D.C.'s budget. How would you spend the taxpayers' money?
SEE: Chapter Seven, pages 88, 90.

Create an interview script with a famous person from Washington, D.C.!

★ Research various Washingtonians, such as Benjamin Banneker, Clara Barton, Elizabeth Keckley, Constantino Brumidi, Duke Ellington, Edward W. Brooke III, and Katharine Graham.

★ Based on your research, pick one person you would most like to talk with.

★ Write a script of the interview. What questions would you ask? How would this person answer? Create a question-and-answer format. You may want to supplement this writing project with a voice-recording dramatization of the interview.

SEE: Chapters Three, Four, Six, Seven, and Eight, pages 33, 51, 52, 81, 84, 89, and 101, and the Biographical Dictionary, pages 133–137.

ART PROJECTS

Create a PowerPoint Presentation or Visitors' Guide

Welcome to Washington, D.C.!

Washington, D.C., is a great place to visit and to live! From its natural beauty to its historic sites, there's plenty to see and do. In your PowerPoint presentation or brochure, highlight 10 to 15 of the district's fascinating landmarks. Be sure to include:

★ a map of the district showing where these sites are located

★ photos, illustrations, Web links, natural history facts, geographic stats, climate and weather, plants and wildlife, and recent discoveries

   SEE: Chapter Nine, pages 102–115, and Fast Facts, pages 126–127.

Design a Memorial

Washington, D.C., has many examples of memorials and monuments. Learn about them and design your own.

★ Research the lives of the artists who designed the memorials and monuments in Washington, D.C. What inspired them?

★ Think about a person or event that could be honored with a monument. Whom or what would you choose?

★ Draw plans for the monument and write a report about the person or event that is important to you.

Research the District of Columbia's Quarter

From 1999 to 2008, the U.S. Mint introduced new quarters commemorating each of the 50 states in the order that they were admitted to the Union. Each state's quarter features a unique design on its reverse, or back. In 2009, the U.S. Mint released a quarter for the District of Columbia.

★ Research the significance of the image. Who designed the quarter? Who chose the final design?

★ Design your own Washington, D.C., quarter. What images would you choose for the reverse?

★ Make a poster showing the Washington, D.C., quarter and label each image.

   GO TO: www.factsfornow.scholastic.com. Enter the keywords **Washington D.C.** and look for the link to the Washinton, D.C., quarter.

SCIENCE, TECHNOLOGY, ENGINEERING, & MATH PROJECTS

Graph Population Statistics!

★ Compare population statistics (such as ethnic background, birth, death, and literacy rates) in Washington, D.C., neighborhoods.

★ In your graph or chart, look at population density and write sentences describing what the population statistics show; graph one set of population statistics and write a paragraph explaining what the graphs reveal.

SEE: Chapter Six, pages 72–75.

Create a Weather Map of Washington, D.C.!

Use your knowledge of Washington, D.C.'s geography to research and identify conditions that result in specific weather events. What is it about the geography of Washington, D.C., that makes it vulnerable to things like thunderstorms and heavy rainfall? Create a weather map or poster that shows the weather patterns over the district. Include a caption explaining the technology used to measure weather phenomena, and provide data.

SEE: Chapter One, page 13.

Track Endangered Species

Using your knowledge of Washington, D.C.'s wildlife, research what animals and plants are endangered or threatened.

★ Find out what the district is doing to protect these species.

★ Chart known populations of the animals and plants, and report on changes in certain geographic areas.

SEE: Chapter One, page 17.

Dwarf wedgemussel

PRIMARY VS. SECONDARY SOURCES

What's the Diff?

Your teacher may require at least one or two primary sources and one or two secondary sources for your assignment. So, what's the difference between the two?

★ **Primary sources are original.** You are reading the actual words of someone's diary, journal, letter, autobiography, or interview. Primary sources can also be photographs, maps, prints, cartoons, news/film footage, posters, first-person newspaper articles, drawings, musical scores, and recordings. By the way, when you conduct a survey, interview someone, shoot a video, or take photographs to include in a project, you are creating primary sources!

★ **Secondary sources are what you find in encyclopedias, textbooks, articles, biographies, and almanacs.** These are written by a person or group of people who tell about something that happened to someone else. Secondary sources also recount what another person said or did. This book is an example of a secondary source.

Now that you know what primary sources are—where can you find them?

★ **Your school or local library:** Check the library catalog for collections of original writings, government documents, musical scores, and so on. Some of this material may be stored on microfilm.

★ **Historical societies:** These organizations keep historical documents, photographs, and other materials. Staff members can help you find what you are looking for. History museums are also great places to see primary sources firsthand.

★ **The Internet:** There are lots of sites that have primary sources you can download and use in a project or assignment.

TIMELINE

★ ★ ★

U.S. Events

Washington, D.C., Events

10,000 BCE

c. 10,000 BCE
The first humans reach the Potomac River.

2000 BCE

c. 2000 BCE
People begin carving bowls from soapstone.

1300 CE

c. 1300 CE
Cooling temperatures drive northern Indians to the Potomac region, leading to warfare.

1400

Corn

1492
Christopher Columbus and his crew sight land in the Caribbean Sea.

1500

1565
Spanish admiral Pedro Menéndez de Avilés founds St. Augustine, Florida, the oldest continuously occupied European settlement in the continental United States.

1600

John Smith

1607
The first permanent English settlement in North America is established at Jamestown.

1608
John Smith sails up the Potomac River.

1620
Pilgrims found Plymouth Colony, the second permanent English settlement.

1632
Henry Fleet establishes a trading post on the Potomac River.

1634
Settlers from two ships, the *Ark* and the *Dove*, establish the English colony of Maryland.

U.S. Events

1776
Thirteen American colonies declare their independence from Great Britain

1787
The U.S. Constitution is written.

1803
The Louisiana Purchase almost doubles the size of the United States.

1812–15
The United States and Great Britain fight the War of 1812.

1846–48
The United States fights a war with Mexico over western territories in the Mexican War.

Smithsonian Institution

1863
President Abraham Lincoln frees all slaves in the Southern Confederacy with the Emancipation Proclamation.

1866
The U.S. Congress approves the Fourteenth Amendment to the U.S. Constitution, granting citizenship to African Americans.

1700

Washington, D.C., Events

1751
The port of Georgetown is founded on the Potomac.

1790
President George Washington selects the site for Washington, D.C.

1800

1800
Congress and the president move into Washington, making it the official seat of government.

1814
British troops burn Washington during the War of 1812.

1848
Work begins on the Washington Monument.

1850
The Compromise of 1850 ends the sale of slaves in Washington.

1855
The Smithsonian Institution Castle opens to the public.

1861–65
Washington serves as a supply station for the Union army during the Civil War.

1865
Abraham Lincoln is assassinated at Ford's Theatre.

1874
Congress ends home rule in Washington.

George Washington

U.S. Events

Washington, D.C., Events

1917–18

The United States engages in World War I.

1922

The Lincoln Memorial is dedicated.

1929

The stock market crashes, plunging the United States more deeply into the Great Depression.

1932

Veterans come to Washington demanding their bonuses.

1939

Marian Anderson gives a concert at the Lincoln Memorial after being refused permission to perform at Constitution Hall.

Marian Anderson

1941–45

The United States engages in World War II.

1944

Delegates from powerful nations meet in Washington to plan the United Nations.

1950–53

The United States engages in the Korean War.

1961

Washington, D.C., residents gain the right to vote in presidential elections.

1963

Martin Luther King Jr. delivers his "I Have a Dream" speech at the Lincoln Memorial.

1964–73

The United States engages in the Vietnam War.

1973

Congress reinstates home rule for Washington.

1976

The first section of the Washington Metro opens.

1991

The United States and other nations engage in the brief Persian Gulf War against Iraq.

1996

Archaeologists discover ancient jewelry in the Foggy Bottom neighborhood.

2000

2001

Terrorists attack the United States on September 11.

2003

The United States and coalition forces invade Iraq.

2008

The United States elects its first African American president, Barack Obama.

2010

Congress passes the Affordable Care Act.

GLOSSARY

★ ★ ★

abolition a legal end to slavery

amendment a change to a law or legal document

Bill of Rights a document listing the first ten amendments, or changes, to the U.S. Constitution

coalition an organization formed by bringing together delegates from several groups

endangered at risk of becoming extinct

exotic foreign; from other places

foundry a building where metals are cast

genocides systematic destructions of national, racial, political, or cultural groups

gothic a style of architecture that features pointed arches

home rule the right of a city, state, or nation to elect its own government

immunity protection against disease

indentured servants people who work for others under contract

magma melted rock that has not yet erupted

metamorphic describing rocks that have been changed by extreme pressure, wind, and water

miasmas thick, clammy mists hanging over a marsh

militia an army made up of citizens trained to serve as soldiers in an emergency

relief financial support given to people in need

rotunda a large, round room

seceded withdrew

segregation separation from others, according to race, class, ethnic group, religion, or other factors

Soviet Union a large nation in eastern Europe and northern and central Asia that formed in 1922 and broke apart into many different countries, including Russia, in 1991

stocks shares in the ownership of a company

suffragists people who campaigned for women's right to vote

surveyor someone whose job is to find the shape and position of an area of land

tributary a river that flows into a larger river

tribute gifts given to a leader in exchange for protection

FAST FACTS

★ ★ ★

District Symbols

Founding date Chosen as the site of the capital city in 1791
Origin of name In honor of President George Washington
and Christopher Columbus
Nickname The Nation's Capital, Capital City
Motto *Justitia Omnibus* ("Justice for All")
Bird Wood thrush
Flower American beauty rose
Tree Scarlet oak

Geography

Total area 68 square miles (177 sq km)
Land 61 square miles (158 sq km)
Water 7 square miles (18 sq km)
Inland water 7 square miles (18 sq km)
Geographic center Near 4th and L Streets NW
Latitude 38°50' to 39°00' N
Longitude 76°50' to 77°10' W
Highest point Point Reno at Fort Reno Park, 409 feet (125 m)
Lowest point Potomac River at sea level

District seal

Population

Population; rank (2010 census)	601,723; 50th
Density (2010 census)	9,856.5 persons per square mile (3,805 per sq km)
Population distribution (2010 census)	100% urban, 0% rural
Ethnic distribution (2010 census)	Black persons: 50.0%
	White persons: 34.8%
	Persons of Hispanic or Latino origin: 9.1%
	Asian persons: 3.5%
	Persons reporting two or more races: 2.1%
	American Indian and Alaska Native persons: 0.2%
	Persons of a different race: 0.2%

Weather

Record high temperature	106°F (41°C) in 1930
Record low temperature	−15°F (−26°C) in 1899
Average July temperature	80°F (27°C)
Average January temperature	36°F (2°C)
Average yearly precipitation	44 inches (112 cm)

District flag

NATURAL AREAS AND HISTORIC SITES

National Historic Sites

Carter G. Woodson Home National Historic Site is the home of Carter G. Woodson, an African American historian, author, and journalist who founded Black History Month.

Ford's Theatre National Historic Site is where President Abraham Lincoln was assassinated.

Frederick Douglass National Historic Site is the 19th-century home of Douglass, a humanitarian and leader in the civil rights movement.

Mary McLeod Bethune Council House National Historic Site honors Bethune's work to educate African Americans and to try to end discrimination.

Pennsylvania Avenue National Historic Site commemorates the street at the heart of the nation's capital.

Sewall-Belmont House National Historic Site is dedicated to the history of the fight for woman suffrage and equal rights.

National Memorials

Washington, D.C., has dozens of national memorials, each commemorating an important event or honoring national heroes. Among the city's memorials are the *African American Civil War Museum; Franklin Delano Roosevelt Memorial; George Mason Memorial; John Ericsson National Memorial; Korean War Veterans Memorial; Lincoln Memorial; Lyndon Baines Johnson Memorial Grove on the Potomac; National Japanese American Memorial to Patriotism During World War II; National World War II Memorial; Theodore Roosevelt Island National Memorial; Thomas Jefferson Memorial; United States Navy Memorial;* and the *Vietnam Veterans Memorial.*

National Monument

One of the city's most recognized monuments is the *Washington Monument,* a 555-foot-tall (169 m) tower with an observatory at the top from which tourists can see all around.

National Parkways

Two national parkways run through the city: the *Baltimore-Washington National Parkway* and the *George Washington Memorial Parkway.*

National Scenic Trail

Crossing through Washington, D.C.'s city limits is the *Potomac Heritage National Scenic Trail*, a 830-mile (1,335 km) path that joins parts of Pennsylvania to the Tidewater area of the Potomac.

Other National Park Service Sites

President's Park includes the White House, the president's residence.

The Franklin Delano Roosevelt Memorial, located along Cherry Tree Walk, near the National Mall

SPORTS TEAMS

★ ★ ★

NCAA Teams (Division I)

American University *Eagles*
George Washington University *Colonials*
Georgetown University *Hoyas*
Howard University *Bison*

PROFESSIONAL SPORTS TEAMS

★ ★ ★

Major League Baseball

Washington *Nationals*

National Hockey League

Washington *Capitals*

National Basketball Association

Washington *Wizards*

Women's National Basketball Association

Washington *Mystics*

National Football League

Washington *Redskins*

Major League Soccer

D.C. *United*

CULTURAL INSTITUTIONS

Libraries

The *Library of Congress*, founded in 1800, is the official library of the United States, serving the U.S. Congress, other parts of government, and the general public.

The *Martin Luther King Jr. Memorial Library*, the main building of the District of Columbia Public Library, has a large mural depicting the life of Martin Luther King Jr. and his influence on the civil rights movement.

The *Folger Shakespeare Library* contains the world's largest collection of information about William Shakespeare.

Museums

The *Smithsonian Institution* is a group of government museums and research centers that include the National Museum of American History, the National Air and Space Museum, the National Museum of the American Indian, the National Gallery of Art, and the National Museum of Natural History.

The *U.S. Holocaust Memorial Museum* is dedicated to providing information on the Holocaust and the millions of men, women, and children killed by the Nazis during World War II.

The *National Women's History Museum* honors women throughout the history of the world.

Performing Arts

The *National Symphony Orchestra*, founded in 1931, performs classical programs and pops concerts at the renowned John F. Kennedy Center for the Performing Arts.

The *Washington National Opera*, founded in 1956, stages performances of classical works and new and rarely performed compositions.

Universities and Colleges

In 2011, the city had 2 public and 18 private institutions of higher learning.

ANNUAL EVENTS

January–March

Three Kings Day Celebration (January)

Dr. Martin Luther King Jr.'s Birthday (January 15)

Chinese New Year Parade (February)

Abraham Lincoln's Birthday Celebration (February)

George Washington's Birthday Celebration (February)

Frederick Douglass Birthday Tribute (February)

D.C. Spring Antiques Fair (March)

Blossom Kite Festival (March)

St. Patrick's Day Parade (March)

April–June

Annual White House Easter Egg Roll (March or April)

White House Spring Garden Tour (April)

National Cherry Blossom Festival in the Tidal Basin (April)

ZooFari (May)

Annual Capital Jazz Fest (June)

Annual National Capital Barbecue Battle (June)

Smithsonian Folklife Festival (June–July)

July–September

Fourth of July Fireworks Display

Annual Capital Hip Hop Soul Fest (July)

Fiesta DC (September)

Library of Congress National Book Festival (September)

Colonial Market and Fair at Mount Vernon (September)

International Children's Festival (September)

October–December

Apple Harvest Festival (October)

Taste of D.C. (October)

Fall Harvest Family Days (October)

Columbus Day Parade (October)

National Christmas Tree Lighting (December)

Washington Jewish Film Festival (December)

Henry Adams (1838–1918) was a novelist and historian who lived much of his life in Washington, D.C. His novel *Democracy* is an account of politics and high society in the capital.

Louisa May Alcott (1832–1888) was a novelist whose works include *Little Women*. During the Civil War, she moved to Washington, D.C., to help care for sick and wounded soldiers. In 1863, she described her experiences in a book called *Hospital Sketches*.

Marian Anderson See page 63.

Pearl Bailey (1918–1990) was an award-winning actress and singer. A graduate of Georgetown University, she starred in Broadway musicals and frequently appeared in films, television, and on radio.

Benjamin Banneker See page 33.

Joel Barlow (1754–1812) was an early American poet. He wrote his major work, *The Columbiad*, while living near today's Rock Creek Park.

Clara Barton See page 51.

Ann Beattie (1947–) is a novelist and short-story writer. She was born in Washington, D.C., and graduated from American University. Her books include *Chilly Scenes of Winter* (1976), *Picturing Will* (1990), and *Park City: New and Selected Stories* (1998).

Alexander Graham Bell (1847–1922), the inventor of the telephone, moved to Washington, D.C., in 1879. He served as president of the National Geographic Society from 1896 to 1904.

Melissa Belote (1956–) is a swimmer who won three gold medals at the 1972 Olympic Games. She was born in Washington, D.C.

Carl Bernstein (1944–), born in Washington, D.C., is a journalist best known for his reporting on the Watergate scandal in the early 1970s. Bernstein and Bob Woodward exposed the scandal in a series of articles in the *Washington Post*. Their reports led to the resignation of President Richard M. Nixon.

Mary McLeod Bethune (1875–1955) was an educator who advised Franklin Roosevelt and several other presidents about issues related to African Americans. Her home in Washington's Logan Circle neighborhood is today a national historic site.

Mary McLeod Bethune

Edward W. Brooke III See page 89.

Chuck Brown See page 83.

Constantino Brumidi See page 81.

Warren Buffett (1930–) is one of the most successful financial investors of the 20th century. Raised in Washington, D.C., he is one of the world's wealthiest people and one of the world's biggest contributors to international charities.

Frances Hodgson Burnett See page 79.

Chris Carmack (1980–) is an American actor and fashion model who has appeared on the television show *The O.C.* He was born in Washington, D.C.

Dave Chappelle

Dave Chappelle (1973–) is a comedian known best for his hit Comedy Central television show, *Chappelle's Show*. He was born in Washington, D.C.

Connie Chung (1946–), a native of Washington, D.C., is an award-winning television journalist.

Roy Clark (1933–) is a country music performer who plays banjo, fiddle, guitar, and harmonica. From 1969 to 1992, he hosted the popular TV variety show *Hee Haw*. He grew up in southeast Washington, D.C.

Stephen Colbert (1964–) is best known as the host of Comedy Central's *The Colbert Report*, a nightly satirical news show. Born in Washington, D.C., he was a performer and an Emmy Award–winning writer on *The Daily Show with Jon Stewart* from 1997 to 2006.

Anna Julia Cooper See page 64.

Benjamin Oliver Davis Jr. (1912–2002) was the first African American general officer in the U.S. Air Force. He was the commander of the famed Tuskegee Airmen, a group of black pilots who flew bomber missions over Europe in World War II. Davis was born in Washington, D.C.

Frederick Douglass See page 115.

Charles Drew (1904–1950) was a physician who developed improved techniques for storing blood. He used his discoveries to set up huge blood banks in World War II, which allowed army doctors to save thousands of American lives. Drew was born in Washington, D.C.

Allen Drury (1918–1998) was a novelist who wrote about power and politics in Washington, D.C. His novel *Advise and Consent* won the Pulitzer Prize in 1960.

John Foster Dulles (1888–1959), who was born in Washington, D.C., was a statesman who helped establish the United Nations. He served as secretary of state under President Dwight D. Eisenhower.

Paul Laurence Dunbar (1872–1906) was a prominent poet who lived in Washington, D.C., from 1898 to 1904 and worked for a year at the Library of Congress. His poems describe the African American experience and are written in the language of ordinary working people.

Kevin Durant (1988–) is a standout shooting guard for the NBA's Oklahoma City Thunder. He was born in Washington, D.C.

Andrew Ellicott (1754–1820) was a land surveyor who completed Pierre-Charles L'Enfant's design for the nation's capital city.

Duke Ellington (1899–1974), who was born in Washington, D.C., was one of the most influential jazz composers and musicians in history. He won multiple Grammy Awards and was awarded the Presidential Medal of Freedom in 1969.

Henry Fleet (1600?–1660) was a fur trader who, in 1632, established the first European outpost on the site of today's Washington, D.C.

Marvin Gaye

Jonathan Safran Foer (1977–) is a writer who was born and raised in Washington, D.C. He has published numerous short stories and two novels: *Everything Is Illuminated* and *Extremely Loud and Incredibly Close*.

Marvin Gaye (1939–1984) was one of the greatest soul singers of all time. He was born in Washington, D.C.

Al Gore (1948–) was the vice president under U.S. president Bill Clinton from 1993 to 2001. Born in Washington, D.C., he had earlier served as a representative and senator from Tennessee in Congress. Today, he is best known as an environmental activist, and he received the Nobel Peace Prize for his work in climate change activism.

Katharine Graham See page 101.

Goldie Hawn (1945–) is a comedic actor who was born in Washington, D.C. She launched her film career in *Cactus Flower* in 1969. Her many hit films include *Private Benjamin* and *Death Becomes Her.*

Goldie Hawn

Helen Hayes (1900–1993) was a Washington-born actor who is sometimes called the First Lady of the American Theater. Her stage and film career spanned nearly 70 years. The Helen Hayes Awards were named in her honor and are presented to outstanding theaters in the D.C. area.

Katherine Heigl (1978–) is an actor who was born in Washington, D.C. She is known for her starring roles in TV's *Grey's Anatomy* and films such as *Wish Upon a Star* and *27 Dresses.*

J. Edgar Hoover (1895–1972) was the founder of the Federal Bureau of Investigation (FBI) and was its director for nearly 50 years. He was born in Washington, D.C.

Langston Hughes (1902–1967) was a poet and essayist who wrote about the African American experience in the United States. In 1924, he moved to Washington, D.C., where he worked briefly for the *Journal of Negro History.*

William Hurt (1950–) is an Academy Award–winning actor who was born in Washington, D.C. His films include *Lost in Space* and *Tuck Everlasting.*

William Hurt

Samuel L. Jackson

Samuel L. Jackson (1948–) is an award-winning actor who was born in Washington, D.C. He has appeared in many of Hollywood's biggest blockbuster hits, including several of the Star Wars movies.

Walter Perry Johnson (1887–1946), a professional baseball player, was considered by many to be the greatest pitcher who ever lived. He won 416 games for the Washington Senators and became a member of the Baseball Hall of Fame in 1936.

Al Jolson (1886–1950) was born Asa Yoelson in Russia and immigrated to Washington, D.C., as a young boy. In the 1930s, he was America's most famous and highest-paid entertainer. He is best known as the star of *The Jazz Singer* (1927), the first "talking motion picture."

Elizabeth Keckley See page 52.

Byron Leftwich (1980–) is an NFL quarterback who has played for the Jacksonville Jaguars and the Atlanta Falcons. He was born in Washington, D.C.

Pierre-Charles L'Enfant (1754–1825) created the original plans for the city of Washington, D.C., but was eventually fired from the project.

Thurgood Marshall (1908–1993) worked in Washington, D.C., as legal counsel to the National Association for the Advancement of Colored People (NAACP). He successfully argued the 1954 Supreme Court case, *Brown v. Board of Education of Topeka*, which barred racial segregation in public schools. He was the first African American appointed to the U.S. Supreme Court, serving from 1967 to 1991.

Robert McNeill (1917–2005), a native of Washington, D.C., was a photographer. His photos of African Americans in Washington, D.C., and Virginia from the 1930s to the 1950s showed the segregation and racism of mid-20th-century America.

Christopher Meloni (1961–) is an actor known for his role on the television series *Law & Order: Special Victims Unit*. He was born in Washington, D.C.

Eleanor Holmes Norton See page 93.

Bill Nye (1955–), who was born in Washington, D.C., is a science educator who had a hit television show called *Bill Nye the Science Guy*.

Marjorie Kinnan Rawlings (1896–1953), was an author who wrote about rural themes and settings. She is best known for her novel *The Yearling*, a story about a boy who adopts a fawn, for which she won the 1939 Pulitzer Prize for Fiction. She was born in Washington, D.C.

Vinnie Ream See page 82.

Chita Rivera (1933–) is a dancer and actor who was born in Washington, D.C. She starred in Broadway hits including *Bye Bye Birdie* and *West Side Story*.

Pete Sampras

John Philip Sousa (1854–1932) was a composer who was born and raised in Washington, D.C. His compositions include "The Washington Post" march and "The Stars and Stripes Forever." He conducted the Marine Corps Band from 1880 to 1892.

Gabrielle Tayac (1967–) is a historian at the Smithsonian Institution's National Museum of the American Indian. She is dedicated to preserving the traditions of Native Americans across the country.

Walt Whitman (1819–1892) is among the greatest American poets. He spent several years in Washington, D.C., during and after the Civil War. He wrote some of his best-known poems, including "O Captain! My Captain!" and "When Lilacs Last in the Dooryard Bloom'd," during these years.

Jeffrey Wright (1965–) is a film and stage actor who was born and raised in Washington, D.C. He appeared in films including *Celebrity* and starred as Martin Luther King Jr. in *Boycott*.

Henry Rollins (1961–) was the lead singer of the bands Black Flag and Rollins Band. Since then, he has hosted television shows and appeared in films. A native Washingtonian, Rollins is active in politics, working to end world hunger and protecting the rights of minority groups.

Pete Sampras (1971–) is a champion tennis player who was born in Washington, D.C. He was the youngest male winner of the U.S. Open at age 19, and he earned 14 Grand Slam titles during his career.

Alexander Shepherd (1835–1902) was head of Washington's Board of Public Works and made important improvements to the city.

John Sirica (1904–1992) spent his childhood in Connecticut and moved to Washington, D.C., to attend boarding school in 1918. He became a judge in the District of Columbia and presided over the trial of the five burglars who were caught breaking into Democratic headquarters at the Watergate Hotel. Nineteen officials in President Richard Nixon's administration were convicted.

Yeardley Smith (1964–) is an actor who was raised in Washington, D.C. She is best known as the voice of Lisa in the long-running TV series *The Simpsons*.

Jeffrey Wright

RESOURCES

★ ★ ★

BOOKS

Nonfiction

House, Katherine L. *The White House for Kids: A History of a Home, Office and National Symbol, With 21 Activities*. Chicago: Chicago Review Press, 2014.

Johnson, Robin. *Famous People of the War of 1812*. New York: Crabtree Publishing Company, 2012.

Krensky, Stephen. *Clara Barton*. New York: DK Publishing, 2011.

Krull, Kathleen. *What Was the March on Washington?* New York: Grosset & Dunlap, 2013.

Mooney, Carla. *George Washington: 25 Great Projects You Can Build Yourself*. White River Junction, Vt.: Nomad Press, 2010.

Ogintz, Eileen. *The Kid's Guide to Washington, DC*. Guilford, Conn.: GPP Travel, 2012.

Rhatigan, Joe. *White House Kids: The Perks, Pleasures, Problems, and Pratfalls of the Presidents' Children*. Watertown, Mass.: Charlesbridge Publishing, 2012.

Fiction

Cabot, Meg. *Ready or Not: An All-American Girl Novel*. New York: HarperCollins, 2005.

Lasky, Kathryn. *A Time for Courage: The Suffragette Diary of Kathleen Bowen*. New York: Scholastic, 2002.

Osborne, Mary Pope. *After the Rain: Virginia's Civil War Diary*. New York: Scholastic, 2002.

Tayac, Gabrielle. *Meet Naiche: A Native Boy from the Chesapeake Bay Area*. Hillsboro, Ore.: Beyond Words Publishing, 2002.

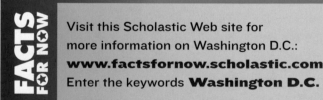

FACTS FOR NOW

Visit this Scholastic Web site for more information on Washington D.C.: **www.factsfornow.scholastic.com** Enter the keywords **Washington D.C.**

INDEX

★ ★ ★

AUTHOR'S TIPS AND SOURCE NOTES

★ ★ ★

Several books on Washington proved valuable in my research. Among them are *Black Men Built the Capitol: Discovering African American History in and Around Washington, D.C.,* by Jesse J. Holland; and *Washington, D.C., 1963–2006,* and *Washington, D.C., 1861–1962,* both by Tracey Gold Bennett.